Textiles
from
Burma

Textiles
from Burma

Featuring the James Henry Green Collection

Edited by Elizabeth Dell and Sandra Dudley

Philip Wilson Publishers

in association with

The James Green Centre for World Art, Brighton

First published in 2003 by Philip Wilson Publishers
7 Deane House, 27 Greenwood Place, London NW5 1LB

In association with the James Green Centre for World Art
at the Royal Pavilion, Libraries & Museums, Brighton,
4-5 Pavilion Buildings, Brighton, BN1 1EE

A catalogue record for this book is available from the British Library

ISBN 0 85667 569 5
ISBN 1 58886 067 1 (Art Media Resources edition)
ISBN 1 932476 05 9 (Buppha Press edition)

Distributed throughout the UK, Europe and the rest of the World excluding North America,
Asia and India by
I.B. Tauris & Co. Ltd
6 Salem Road, London W2 4BU

Published in the USA by Art Media Resources, Inc.
Chicago Illinois
info@artmediaresources.com
www.artmediaresources,com

Published for distribution in Asia (excluding India) by
Buppha Press, PO Box 10335 Chicago, IL 60610

Published in India by
Timeless Books, 46 Housing Society, South Extension Part-1,
New Delhi-110049, India

Editors Elizabeth Dell & Sandra Dudley
Designer Nigel Cunningham

Printed and bound in Spain by Mateu Cromo Artes Graficas, Madrid

Book jacket: Skirtcloth (labu). Kachin, Jinghpaw, southern Kachin State and northern Shan states, c.1900. Cotton and wool, three bands with discontinuous supplementary weft. 1770 mm x 750 mm.
Royal Pavilion, Libraries & Museums G000015
Back jacket: Maran Kai Htang works on a Htingnai wedding outfit for Brighton Museum, Myitkyina 2002. Photograph by Salaw Zau Ring, B0077.
Endpapers: Skirtcloth (labu) – back detail. Kachin, Jinghpaw Sinli and Jinghpaw Gauri, southern Kachin State and northern Shan states, c.1900. Cotton and goats' wool, 3 bands with supplementary weft. 1630 mm x 630 mm.
Royal Pavilion, Libraries & Museums G000022
Half-title: Demonstrating how a La:cid Ngawchang jacket is worn, Myitkyina 1999. Photograph by Elizabeth Dell.
Frontispiece: Woman's jacket. Kachin, La:cid Ngawchang, made in Myitkyina c.1997 by Hkaw Nyaw. Made from handspun indigo-dyed cotton.
Royal Pavilion, Libraries & Museums WA508297

Photographic credits:
Royal Pavilion, Libraries & Museums textiles photographed by John Williams

Fig.2.vii and Fig.2.ix. By permission of the Pitt Rivers Museum.
Fig.4.6.ii Stole. Private collection.
Chapter 4.3 and 6.1. Chin textiles, Hollander collection, photographed by Ralph Koch.
Chapter 5, Fig.5.1.ii – Fig.5.1.vi. By permission of the Victoria & Albert Museum.
Fig.5.2.1 Scherman photograph, 1910. © St Gallen Museum.
Fig.6.2.ii photograph. By permission of Eleanor Gaudoin.
Fig.6.2.vii photograph. By permission of Sao Hkam Hip Hpa.
Fig.6.2.viii photograph. By permission of Janet Browne.

Contents

Foreword

Formed whilst working as a recruiting and intelligence officer in Burma during the 1920s and 1930s, James Henry Green's collection offers a vivid glimpse into a particular place and time. His exceptional collection of photographs shows a wide range of landscapes and people: colonial officers, strangers, friends and family. His collection of books, articles, diaries and fieldnotes offers a context in which to frame these individuals and the beautiful textiles, which frequently reveal the signs of wear, convey an impression of human contact. These sources together give us a compelling sense of life in Burma in the early part of the twentieth century.

Brighton Museum and Art Gallery is extremely fortunate to be the caretaker of Green's collection and the recipient of financial support from the James Green Charitable Trust. The generosity of the Trust has enabled the Museum to use Green's collections as the starting point for building new links between Burma and Britain, Green's time and our own. These links have sparked exciting exchanges between museum professionals, researchers, students and individuals both here and in Burma.

We hope this book will reflect some of the many dialogues that have informed the development of the Green textile collection and will open the platform for many more. There are a number of people to whom I would like to extend thanks, not least to those individuals in Burma who have contributed their expertise, experience and enthusiasm.

I would also like to thank the following people: Oonagh Connolly, Susan Conway, Caroline Cook, Sadan Ja Ngai, Patricia Herbert, Lisa Maddigan, Penny Marlow, Rebecca Quinton, Hkanhpa Tu Sadan, Mandy Sadan, Catherine Speight and Louise Tythacott, for their work on Green's textile collection; contributors, John Barker, Elizabeth Dell, Sandra Dudley, Frances Franklin, Sylvia Fraser-Lu, Ralph Isaacs, Vibha Joshi, Lisa Maddigan, Mandy Sadan and Mika Toyota for their professionalism and zeal and, especially, Sandra Dudley for her assiduous editorial work; also, Nigel Cunningham for design and John Williams for photography.

This book would not have been possible without the support of the Open Society Institute. We are grateful also to museum colleagues around the world for their valuable assistance and to those institutions that generously allowed us to use images of items in their collections.

Lastly I would like to thank Elizabeth Dell, Keeper of World Art and Anthropology and Head of the Green Centre, and Helen Mears, Curator of World Art, for overseeing this publication and to the Trustees of the James Henry Green Charitable Trust for their continuing enthusiasm and support for the Green Centre's work.

Jessica Rutherford
Head of Libraries and Museums and Director of the Royal Pavilion

Preface

When James Green arrived in Burma in 1918 he found himself in one of the most ethnically and linguistically diverse countries in the whole of Southeast Asia with over 240 languages and dialects spoken and more than 120 distinct groups of people. Green was dazzled by the cultural diversity he saw around him and, like others working at the far reaches of the British Empire, he eagerly turned to the new science of anthropology to provide him with an 'objective' means of recording his new environment.

Green quickly realised that textiles could signify ethnic difference and he wrote detailed notes on the dress and physical appearance of the people he encountered in his recruitment and intelligence work. His notes focus largely on how textiles reflected group identity and sadly, there are few records in his archive that tell us how, where, when and from whom the textile pieces were collected. It is likely that this information would have revealed stories of the personal friendships and relationships that Green formed with the people he met.

In recent work being undertaken on behalf of the James Green Centre for World Art these stories are being retraced by revisiting areas where Green worked. Through initiatives such as the Kachin textile project, which involved commissioning 17 'traditional' wedding outfits in Kachin state, thorough documentation ensures that light is thrown not only on the design, making and significance of the new textiles but also on their historic counterparts. This process also enables the Museum to explore how the traditions of dress recorded by Green in the 1920s are interpreted today and, by commissioning and collecting new textiles in Burma, to support the continuity of contemporary weavers' creativity, skills and traditions.

As the Green collection has grown the wonder of the stylistic range, technical talent, and sheer beauty of Burma's textiles never diminishes. The variation that so struck Green continues to amaze. This book is both an introduction to the production of textiles in Burma and a celebration of the diversity they represent.

John Govett
Chairman, James Henry Green Charitable Trust

Chapter 1

Introduction

Elizabeth Dell and Sandra Dudley

Sumptuous textiles have been produced and worn in great variety by the different peoples living in Burma.[1] Through the centuries, these have inspired the recordings of artists and writers, from votive temple murals, to the documents of awed visitors. Travellers have brought back vivid examples of these textiles to museums and collections around the world. In Burma today (and for its dispersed communities), woven textiles continue to play an important role in defining personal and group identity.

Textiles from Burma explores themes relating to the history, production, meaning, collection and continuing impact of textiles from Burma. It looks at textiles within their local contexts, at court, serving religious ends, underpinning national identity. It investigates textiles in their wider contexts, examining aspects of collecting and documentation in colonial and modern times, exploring the histories and identities that are made and re-made as textiles are collected and written about.

What is presented is not a comprehensive view of textiles from Burma, rather a way of looking at the wider contexts of particular textile traditions. The starting point is the James Henry Green collection of textiles and photographs from Burma. Strengths of this collection from the 1920s and 1930s, or its areas of development in recent years at Brighton Museum, form the starting point for a broader study of Burma textiles. Each thematic case study is underpinned

*Detail: woman's belt, Kachin Jinghpaw
Hkahku, northern Kachin State and Hukawng
valley, collected in the 1920s. The dragon
motif, one of the most difficult patterns to
weave, represents Baren Num Raw in
Jinghpaw mythology, and is a symbol of duwa
(chief) status.
Royal Pavilion, Libraries & Museums
G000210*

9

Jinphaw Kachin Woman
Myitkyina.

Ekaw Woman
Kengtung State.

Shan Chinese Old Man.
Lashio. N.S.S

Padaung Woman.
Toungoo Dist.

Noble Shan Girl.
Kengtung State.

Fig.1.i left
Map of Burma indicating contemporary state boundaries and places featured in the text.

Fig.1.ii above
Watercolour by Yadanabon Maung Su (1903–1965), showing 'Jinphaw [Jinghpaw] Kachin woman, Myitkyina; Ekaw [Akha] Woman, Kengtung State; Shan Chinese Old Man, Lashio, N.S.S [northern Shan State]; Padaung woman, Taungyo district; Noble Shan girl, Kengtung State', 20 May 1958. Royal Pavilion, Libraries & Museums WA508631, donated by Noel F. Singer

by an introduction to the weaving traditions of its particular region, draws variously on archival and/or field research and is supported by fine examples of textiles from collections around the world.

Contexts

Burma has long been characterised by the bewildering diversity of the many upland and lowland groups who live within and straddled across its borders. Each group has its own distinct, dynamic set of traditions, mythology, language, history and social structure. Like people everywhere, all groups continue to develop, change and reinforce their perceptions of themselves, of those with whom they interact locally, and of the wider world and their own place within it. Real and imagined cultural differences between groups play a central part in these perceptions of self and other, and in associated ideas of identity.

Textiles and dress, particularly styles that are increasingly self-consciously considered 'traditional', are perhaps the most immediate, visual component of these cultural differences, for some groups even more so than for others (Fig.1.iii). Indeed, in the past and often still today, dress was and is overly relied upon as a means by which to squeeze people into neat, ethnic pigeonholes with only limited resemblance to a reality in which groups are fluid and blurred around the edges. Moreover, textiles as other 'traditions' were, and often still are, portrayed as fixed and unchanging, rather than the culturally and politically manipulable, dynamic symbols they actually are. As some of our case studies show, perhaps surprisingly, textiles can be integral to current political and humanitarian situations (Fig.1.iv), as well as to the cultural, historical and museological issues also discussed in this volume.

Fig.1.iii

*Kayan Kangkaw ('Padaung') women and
men walking.*

*Photograph by James Henry Green, c.1926.
Royal Pavilion, Libraries & Museums 1446*

To emphasise that 'tradition' is dynamic and manipulable, however, is not to say certain 'traditions' cannot be identified with certain groups, nor that they should not be celebrated. Indeed, one of the purposes of this volume is to explore and rejoice in just a small part of the richness that is Burma textiles.

With some honourable exceptions,[2] little has been written about the range of Burma textiles and dress save normative descriptions in early ethnographies and travel writing. Beyond these, in the past, interest in Burma textiles was restricted mainly to museum documentation and publications of material that had come to be deposited in museums, mainly in Europe and North America. The bulk of Burma textiles in these museums dates from before the middle of the twentieth century. Most items were collected by missionaries (especially material now in North America), colonial officers (predominantly material now in the United Kingdom), and anthropologists, explorers and others (Europe, the United Kingdom and North America). Until recently, museum publications on any sort of object or collection, be it from Burma or elsewhere, did not explicitly locate the collector and museum within the 'life cycle' of the artefacts in question. There was little consideration of how the collector, museum and scholars dealing with the material, before and after it came to the museum, played and continue to play

Fig.1.iv top
Naw Sarah (name changed) weaving a
Karen bag on backstrap loom, Karenni
Refugee Camp 5, 1997.
Photograph by Sandra Dudley.

Fig.1.v above
Woman hanging out freshly dyed and
washed green and red skeins of cotton to dry
in the sun. Thabyei Auk, near Mandalay,
1996.
Photograph by Sandra Dudley.

a part in determining how the artefacts were and are seen and understood, and, in turn, what that might mean for the ways in which the source communities have been perceived by others and by themselves.

This volume does not pretend to be all encompassing in its discussion of these issues. Through its case studies, however, the book seeks both to document further some of the wonderful textiles produced by people from Burma, and, importantly, to situate these textiles within some of the historical, social, cultural, religious, political, museological and academic contexts in which, at various stages in their histories, the textiles might find themselves.

Chapter 2

Green's collections and their historical and present contexts

Detail: skirtcloth (labu). Kachin Jinghpaw Sinli
and Jinghpaw Gauri, southern Kachin State
and northern Shan States, c.1900. See Fig.2.v.

James Henry Green, 1893–1975

Elizabeth Dell

Fig.2.i *above*

'Christmas dinner at Sinlum. Self included.'
James Henry Green enjoying a Christmas
gathering at Sinlum Kaba in the Kachin Hills,
c.1926. This kind of government sponsored
event provided an opportunity for local
officials to meet with a wide variety of
people who would travel in from the
surrounding hills 'dressed in their most
splendid attire.'
Royal Pavilion, Libraries & Museums 0373

Fig.2.ii *below right*

'Chinghpaw [Jinghpaw], Yawyin, Maru and
Lashi women.'
Photograph by James Henry Green, 1920s.
Royal Pavilion, Libraries & Museums 0671

James Henry Green was a military man whose appointment to the Indian Army took him to Burma in 1918, aged 25. His work as a recruiting officer with the Burma Rifles took him to remote northern hill regions, where his role was to identify villages or peoples offering resilient candidates for the army (Fig.2.i). His fascination with the people he met living in this area fed what was to become a lifelong pursuit of anthropology, consolidated in his Fellowship of the Royal Anthropological Institute from 1928.

Green's writing from this time shows he was strongly motivated by an interest in ethnic difference in these hill regions. He studied the nuances of different customs, beliefs, languages and physical attributes that distinguished neighbouring groups, and recorded these according to the anthropological theories of the day. His observations formed the basis of his 1934 dissertation for Cambridge University, 'The Tribes of Upper Burma North of 24° Latitude and their Classification'. The excellence of his military intelligence work was recognised in 1930 in the award of the MacGregor Memorial Medal for exploratory work in the Triangle.

Green's observation of people – for military and anthropological ends – also resulted in an impressive photographic collection. In over 1,600 photographs, taken between 1918 and 1935, Green captured people, customs and places.[1] These images meticulously record dress, ornamentation and physical difference of the mainly Kachin, Shan, Chin, Kayah and Karen peoples among whom

Fig.2.iii

Skirtcloth (labu). Kachin, Jinghpaw Sinli and Jinghpaw Gauri, southern Kachin State and northern Shan States, c.1900. Cotton and wool, three bands with discontinuous supplementary weft, 1390 mm x 1090 mm. Royal Pavilion, Libraries & Museums G000016a

he worked (Fig.2.ii). Some images show detached observation of people whose customs Green found extraordinary, others are intimate portraits of people who were his friends and colleagues.

In 1934, Green married Dorothy McColl, a young Anglo-Burmese woman who had spent much of her childhood in Burma. Green tried to persuade Dorothy that, as a woman, she could make a valuable contribution to the anthropological study that so absorbed him.[2] While there is apparently no evidence of Dorothy's contribution to Green's study, her influence is clear in the textile collection that the couple assembled.

In 1937 Green left Burma for Singapore, and in 1943 left Asia and retired from the army. The remainder of his career was devoted to work at the Foreign Office. While he continued to collect anthropological books and journals and attend international conferences, Green did not pursue his earlier desire to become a professional anthropologist. His archive, photograph and textile collection surrounded him in his Surrey home and following his death in 1975, his widow set about trying to establish a small museum there, in association with the Burma Rifles, which had been so influential in Green's life and collecting.

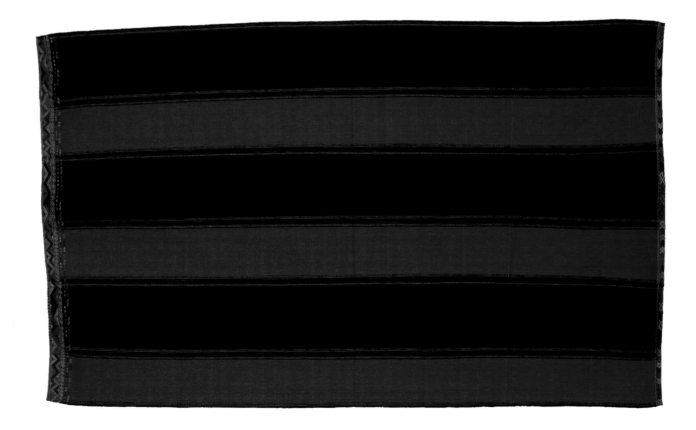

The Green collection at Brighton Museum

Elizabeth Dell

The original Green collection at Brighton comprises about 230 textiles, costumes, dress accessories and weapons, brought together by Green between 1918 and 1935. It is part of a larger collection of photographs, books and ephemera that remained from Green's time in Burma and survived his flight from Singapore at its fall in 1942.

In 1992, this collection was given on long loan to Brighton Museum, with an annual endowment for its research and development: the intention was that over time it would form the core of a substantial body of research and extended collection. In developing this collection, Brighton Museum has taken as its cue the strengths of the existing collection and the need to acquire material that enhances and explicates Green's work. Currently the textile collection numbers some 550 pieces.

Fig.2.v right

Skirtcloth (labu). Kachin, Jinghpaw Sinli and Jinghpaw Gauri, southern Kachin State and northern Shan States, c.1900. Cotton and goats' wool, 3 bands with supplementary weft, 1630 mm x 630 mm.
Royal Pavilion, Libraries & Museums
G000022

Fig.2.iv left

Skirtcloth (labu), Kachin, Jinghpaw Hkahku, northern Kachin State and Hukawng Valley, c.1900. Cotton and wool, 3 bands with supplementary weft, 1890 mm x 1020 mm.
Royal Pavilion, Libraries & Museums
G000020

Fig.2.vi

*Costume accessories. The Brighton Green
Collection includes a range of jewellery,
weapons and accessories worn with the
textiles. Silver, alloys, shells and amber.
Royal Pavilion, Libraries & Museums
G000059a,b, 60a,b, 74–77, 78/79, 82/83,
96/97, 98, 167/168*

The original collection is strong in textiles from the Kachin areas where Green
undertook most of his work with the army. However, it also includes small
numbers of Shan, Karen, Kayah, Burman and Chin textiles. A few of the textiles
and items of clothing were clearly made for Dorothy Green, some of which date
from her childhood in the 1910s.

Green's writing and photography show an earnest attempt to document and
understand the relationship between ethnic difference and its manifestation in
cultural markers such as language and dress. There is little evidence of this
systematic approach in what remains at Brighton of his textile collection. While his
texts carefully record differences in dress from one region to the next, or the
significance of changes in accessories or influences from neighbouring groups, the
textiles collected by him appear to be far more random in distribution. In addition,
while Green's photographs have been systematically indexed by him, and are used
as evidence in his dissertation, the textiles are largely unprovenanced – there is no
indication that he intended them as objects of serious study in their own right.[3]

Green's approach to the documentation of artefacts donated by him to the Pitt
Rivers Museum at Oxford, however, was markedly different.

The Green collection at the Pitt Rivers Museum

Sandra Dudley

Oxford University's Pitt Rivers Museum contains a significant collection of objects acquired in Burma by Green and donated by him to the Museum during his lifetime. This collection comprises four items given in 1929, and approximately 150 given by 1934.

Most of these items are beautifully illustrated in colour sketches done by E. S. Thomas on the Museum's Second World War era catalogue cards. There are, however, only eleven textiles and textile related objects in the collection. Indeed, the majority of the collection comprises weapons, traps and other hunting and fishing equipment, tools, and smoking and betel chewing apparatus. Most are well documented, usually with locations, ethnic groups and often local names provided by Green. The bulk of the collection consists of items collected by Green himself in the northern part of what is now Kachin State, from the Nung, Maru, Jinghpaw, Hkahku and Lisu groups. There are, however, also a number of Shan, Burman, Karen and other items apparently collected in the field by Green. Furthermore, there are some Chin items which may or may not have been collected by Green, including items collected in Maisekan and Padowa villages in the southern Chin hills by the then District Superintendent of Police at Kyaukhpyu.[4]

Fig.2.viii *above*

Jacket. Kachin, Lhaovo: (Maru), Nmai region, northeast Kachin State. Collected in Myitkyina in 1996. Upper part striped indigo and natural cotton, lower part dyed red ?dogs' hair, discontinuous supplementary weft. Edge piped with blue tape. Length 470 mm. Royal Pavilion, Libraries & Museums WA507425

Fig.2.ix *right*

Blanket, Nung-Rawang, Upper Nmai Valley, Kachin State. Undyed hemp, with tufted surface on the underside with blue and red spots and blue, red and black zigzag bands at the edge, beyond which is a broad band of red, black, blue and yellow lozenge pattern with red ?dogs' hair woven ends. Discontinuous supplementary weft. Width 720 mm. Described by Green as 'a valuable object'. Pitt Rivers Museum, University of Oxford 1934.81.92

Fig.2.x

'Nung Myihtoi.' Nung-Rawang spirit medium wearing what is almost certainly a hempen cloth now in the Pitt Rivers Museum (possibly PRM number 1934.81.92).

Photograph by James Henry Green, c.1926.

Royal Pavilion, Libraries & Museums 0048

The textiles and clothes include Jinghpaw and Hkahku bags, and, most importantly, a rare Lhaovo: (Maru) jacket (Fig.2.vii; see also Fig.2.viii) and four Nung hempen items. The latter comprise a blanket with an unusual and striking 'tufted' decorative surface (Fig.2.ix), a bag, and two skirtcloths. There is also a Nung basket used by women for carrying a spindle and thread, and two Ngoru Chin clothing items (a skirt made of grass strips and a raincoat made of leaves).

Fig.2.xi

Man's jacket, leggings, hat and hairpiece. 'Flowery Lisu', Myitkyina, Bhamo and Sadon region, Kachin State. Collected c.1926. Tailored from narrow bands of undyed hemp, with indigo dyed hemp piping and shoulder patches. Length 1030 mm. Royal Pavilion, Libraries & Museums G000033a,b,c and G000091b

Green and textile collecting in the 1920s

Elizabeth Dell

Over the centuries, the textiles produced and worn in great diversity in Burma have inspired artists, writers and photographers in their work. However, aside from examples such as preciously adorned court regalia, textiles have largely remained low value items. Their collection by outsiders has ranged from the systematic assembling of field samples, to the apparently whimsical selecting of souvenirs. Textiles tend to be portable and are easily absorbed into the homes or wardrobes of expatriate collectors. Green's collection, together with the supporting documentation of his archive, gives an insight into the multiple

Fig.2.xii

Woman's jacket and skirt. 'Black Lisu', Putao region, northern Kachin State. Collected c.1926. Jacket tailored from narrow bands of undyed cotton, with weft woven pinstripes. Indigo dyed cotton sleeve borders and undyed cotton lining. Length 590 mm. Circular skirt tailored from long vertical strips, undyed cotton and undyed cotton with weft-woven indigo pinstripes. Red and blue cotton embroidered detail at hem. Length 700 mm. Royal Pavilion, Libraries & Museums G000090a,b

motivations foreigners might have had for amassing textiles. For Green, this ranged from items intended for professional study at the leading anthropological museum of his day (i.e. Nung textiles at the Pitt Rivers), to those collected in sets and apparently used as soft furnishings (i.e. Chin blankets).

At the 'professional' end of this scale was the relationship between the textiles and Green's military and anthropological work. Green was travelling in remote, often unmapped locations, and he was aware that the rarity of his observations and images lent them value. The same applied to his textiles, particularly where he believed he was recording cultures that were threatened by imminent change. As a result, some textiles in Green's collection seem to be part of carefully assembled complete outfits. For example, the male and female Lisu outfits with accessories extending even to human hair plaits, are accompanied by detailed observations on dress and adornment in his dissertation [5] (Fig.2.xi, Fig.2.xii).

Several of the textiles in Green's collection feature in his photographs. It would appear that these are recorded as worn by their original owners, rather than modelled for Green from his collection – for example, the Hkamti Shan shawl worn by the 'Queen of Putao'[6] (Fig.2.xiii, Fig.2.xiv). This relationship between

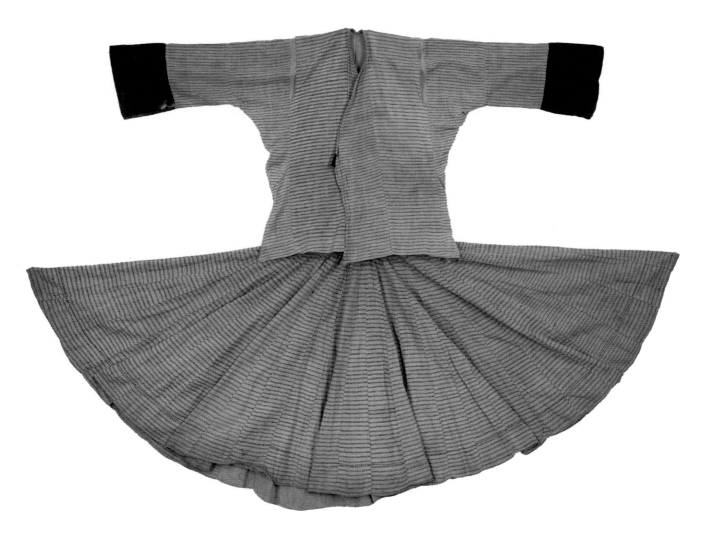

Fig.2.xiv above
'Queen of Putao. Full length.'
Photograph by James Henry Green, c.1926.
Royal Pavilion, Libraries & Museums 0124

Fig.2.xiii above right
Detail of cloth. Hkamti Shan, Hkamti Long,
Putao region, northern Kachin State. Collected
c.1926. Comprises two strips of woven
natural cotton (3740 mm x 480 mm)
stitched together lengthways and folded over
to form a closed 'bag' 1870 mm x 960mm.
Warp and weft stripe decoration to the
edges, and embroidered animal and
geometric motifs to fringed edge. Worn as a
shawl in Green's photograph Fig.2.xiv.
Royal Pavilion, Libraries & Museums
G000025

textiles and individuals brings an element to the collecting of textiles which is absent for collectors of less personal items. With some exceptions, Green's textiles have been used and worn, and carry with them the intimacy of human contact.

Clearly, Green's military position and the relationships formed in the course of his work meant that he had privileged access not only to information and people, but also to artefacts. He would have participated to an extent in the elaborate system of gift exchange which operated in the northern Kachin territories, for example. While he specifically records some gifts such as daggers or swords, it is likely that textiles were also acquired as part of this dialogue. Green's relationship with Burma continued through his life, and this connection also accounted for textile gifts of sentiment brought to Green in England (for example the 'Independent Burma' bag, the gift of Sao Shwe Thaike, who was the first President of Burma. Fig.2.xv).

At the other end of this scale, photographs of the Greens taken in Burma in the 1930s introduce humour and irreverence to their role as collectors, and provide an insight into the fate of many 'exotic' textiles in expatriate hands. In these photographs, the couple pose in fancy dress. Dorothy Green wears the striking Maru skirtcloth and richly decorated jacket, with accessories, and Green's outfit is topped by a wig from the Lisu collection (see Fig.2.xvi).

In some cases, textiles have been slightly modified for use by the Greens, either transformed into hangings, or altered to accommodate European fashion sense and worn by Dorothy Green. However, the majority of the collection appears to have been carefully preserved by the Greens as fine examples of weaving, carried home with them in their flight from Asia, and finally, through their bequest, transformed into museum objects.

Fig.2.xvi *above*
James and Dorothy Green pose in fancy dress, wearing textiles and accessories from their collection. See the Lhaovo: (Maru) skirtcloth G000032b in Fig.2.xix, and the jacket, G000032a also photographed by Green, in Fig.2.xviii. Photographer unknown. Royal Pavilion, Libraries & Museums 1664

Fig.2.xv *right*
Commemorative bag. Shan, northern Shan State. Brown cotton warp and natural and dyed silk weft, with supplementary weft motifs. Text 'Independent Burma' on one side and 'Independent Namkham N.S.S' on the other, with flag motifs. Length, excluding strap and tassels, 250 mm x 240 mm. Given to Green by Sao Shwe Thaike who was the first President of Burma (1948–1952), during an official visit to Britain.
Royal Pavilion, Libraries & Museums G000005

Green, Oxford and anthropology

Sandra Dudley

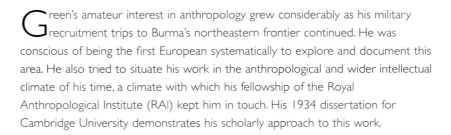

Green's amateur interest in anthropology grew considerably as his military recruitment trips to Burma's northeastern frontier continued. He was conscious of being the first European systematically to explore and document this area. He also tried to situate his work in the anthropological and wider intellectual climate of his time, a climate with which his fellowship of the Royal Anthropological Institute (RAI) kept him in touch. His 1934 dissertation for Cambridge University demonstrates his scholarly approach to this work.

Ethnography was then couched in the ideology of 'science'. Anthropological research was viewed as a scientific endeavour in which physical, racial characteristics and cultural traits could be systematically measured or investigated, and objectively recorded. Motivations included both science for science's sake (the advancement of 'knowledge') and 'salvage ethnography' (recording for posterity the features and cultures of peoples deemed to be 'disappearing' in the face of colonial and modern advances).[7] In his photography, academic contacts and writing, Green, like other professional or amateur anthropologists of his time, seems to have worked within a framework dominated by these twin ideas of science and salvage. Furthermore, anthropologists of this period included many 'professionalised amateurs' like Green: colonial and military officers developing their anthropological interests and collecting ethnographic data that in many cases is still of value today.

Evidence of the detail of Green's contacts in the anthropological and museum worlds of his time is sparse, but it is certain that he did correspond with Oxford's Sir John Linton Myres, an archaeologist who was Honorary Secretary of the RAI in 1900–03 and President in 1928–31. In 1926, Myres promised to ask the RAI about getting measuring equipment for Green to use in the north Burma hills, indicating Green's keenness 'scientifically' to measure physical characteristics and use photography to document physical types and cultural phenomena, including dress (Fig.2.xvii).

The Pitt Rivers Museum's Green collection bears the hallmarks of this attempt at a systematic, 'scientific' approach. The Chin items collected by the District Superintendent of Police at Kyaukhpyu may well have been specially requested by Green as particular specimens for his collection. They include blowpipes, a bow, arrows and fire saws. The Green collection as a whole includes fifteen bows and four blowpipes, and such weapons are and were then one of the Museum's

Fig.2.xvii

Detail of 'Self measuring skulls in Myitkyina.'
Green poses while using anthropological
equipment to measure skulls. The skulls were
probably obtained from a government
expedition to abolish the practice of human
sacrifice and headhunting among the Naga
peoples, 1920s.
Royal Pavilion, Libraries & Museums 1494

collection strengths. Furthermore, fire making equipment was also a particular interest of the then Curator of the Museum, Henry Balfour. Did Green have a correspondence and even friendship with Balfour? No surviving letters have been found, but the suspicion is strong. Why else did Green, later at least a Cambridge man, give systematically amassed collections to the Pitt Rivers Museum rather than to Cambridge University's Museum of Archaeology and Anthropology? Perhaps the explanation lies solely in his relationship with Myres. But whatever the true reasons, the Museum has benefited from acquiring such a coherent and well provenanced collection.

Development of the Green textile collection at Brighton Museum

Lisa Maddigan

Fig.2.xix below

Skirtcloth (labu). Kachin, Lhaovo: (Maru), Nmai region, northeast Kachin State, collected 1920s. Skirt has broad, alternating undyed and indigo dyed cotton warp bands, joined with fine blue, red, navy and natural stripes. Ends finished in dyed red goats' wool bands with supplementary weft details in yellow, blue, red and pink. 1510 mm x 750 mm. This distinctive style of skirtcloth is no longer worn by Lhaovo: (Maru) women, but is more closely resembled by contemporary Nung-Rawang skirtcloth designs (see Fig.2.xx and Fig.2.xxi).

Royal Pavilion, Libraries & Museums G000032b

James Green's textile collection and archive of notes, photographs, maps and reference books provide Brighton Museum with a unique context for exploring the design, production and use of textiles in Burma. The original textile collection and archive offer a fascinating insight into how textiles were made and worn in the 1920s and into how they were seen and collected by Green (Fig.2.xviii, Fig.2.xix). At Brighton Museum today, work on the collection concentrates on bringing these stories to the fore, and on developing the original textile collection with new acquisitions and research projects in the parts of Burma where Green worked, in the border regions of Thailand and China, and in Great Britain.

Fig.2.xviii *right*
'Two Maru Girls'.

Green wrote in his dissertation, 'The women's skirts are longer but of similar design to those of the Nungs and are fastened with the opening on the right. The fancy border of the Nung skirt has been increased to about six inches. In the north two types of skirts are seen: the one is woven in deep blue and white stripes and the other in narrower red, white and blue stripes. In the south white thread is rarely used.'

Photograph by James Henry Green, c.1926.

Royal Pavilion, Libraries & Museums 1034

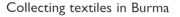

Collecting textiles in Burma

Most of the textiles added to the original Green collection have come from research projects in Southeast Asia. More than 200 textiles were purchased from weavers, shopkeepers and local contacts in Burma and its border regions between 1994 and 1999 (Fig.2.xx). These new acquisitions have enabled the Museum to explore how the traditions of dress recorded by Green in the 1920s are interpreted today, and to continue to build records of textile design and production in Burma (Fig.2.xxi).

Although inspired by the interest that Green took in how dress is used to signify identity in Burma, the Museum's approach to collecting textiles is different (Fig.2.xxii). Green wanted to record how general styles of dress reflect group identity in the Kachin hills, and used this as a way of classifying people. Today, the Museum's interests are focused on individual textiles, and on the individuals who make, wear and sell them. This is reflected in the documentation of the two collections. While Green's archive and dissertation are rich in observations of dress styles, his notes generally make no direct link with the textiles that he collected. For Museum projects today, by contrast, the link between individual textiles and documentation is fundamental, with careful attention paid to how and by whom the piece was made, by whom it would be worn and when, why and how it was acquired. This approach ensures that the acquisition of new pieces for the Green collection is integral to building records of the traditions, methods and choices of design and materials that are shown in a piece of work, alongside its history of ownership.

In 2001, the Green Centre's fieldwork collecting and research policy was revised, placing a strong emphasis on commissioning new work and documentation that directly relates to the existing collections. The Kachin textile project was subsequently set up, benefiting from the strength of contacts built up in Kachin State through Hkanhpa Tu Sadan and Mandy Sadan's ongoing work with the Green collection in Burma. The textile project presented an opportunity to work closely with weavers and local researchers in Kachin State to commission a fully documented collection of textiles and to develop a research resource that would be useful for the Green Centre and for people in Kachin State (Fig.2.xxiii). The project enabled the Museum to promote the importance of recording and preserving cultural heritage in Kachin State, to share archive information held by the Green Centre and to use the acquisitions budget to support contemporary weavers in making new work (Fig.2.xxiv). Documentation of the project, which includes a series of interviews with the weavers, raised interesting issues about developing collecting projects with local researchers and makers (Fig.2.xxv).

While representing a positive direction for developing the Green collection, the process of building shared records needs to balance the interests and preferred methods of the community with those of the Museum. This works towards establishing a mutual understanding of how cultural archives can be developed and used by both. The Museum needs also to consider its role in the development of these projects, and in the dialogues that are initiated by such work. The Kachin textile project highlighted these issues, alongside the importance of contextualising the information that has been recorded.

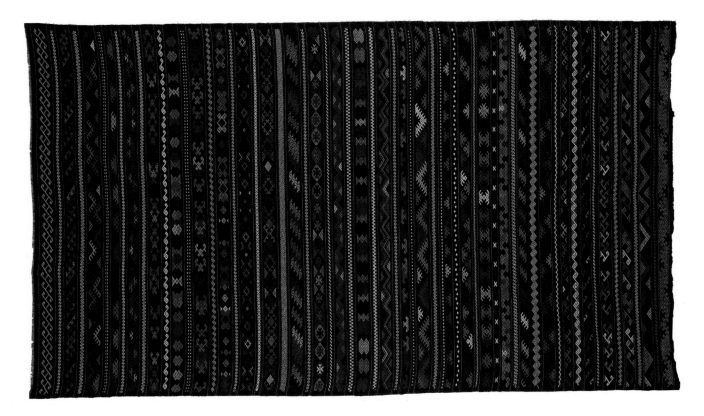

Fig.2.xxiii above

Eight of the weavers who worked on the textile project with Brighton Museum in 2001–2, dressed in traditional Kachin outfits, Myitkyina.
Photograph by Htoi Awng, 2001.
Royal Pavilion, Libraries & Museums B0049

Fig.2.xxi right

Skirtcloth. Kachin, Nung-Rawang, made in Myitkyina in 2002 by Sang Dawng Tang. Woven in three segments in cotton, wool and synthetic thread. Compare this contemporary 'traditional' Nung-Rawang skirtcloth with the Lhaovo: (Maru) skirtcloth collected 80 years previously by Green (Fig.2.xix).
830 mm x 980 mm.
Royal Pavilion, Libraries & Museums WA508793

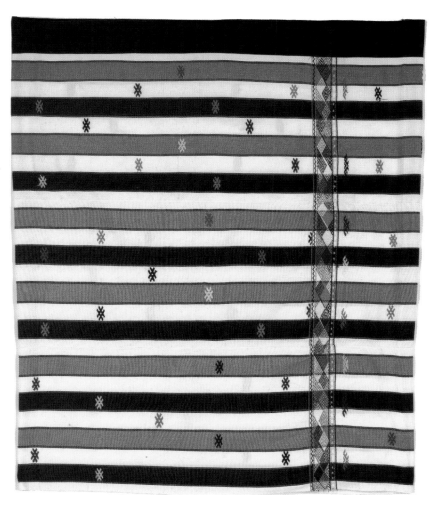

Collecting textiles in Brighton

In Great Britain, the Museum focuses on collecting textiles that have been kept by people from Burma who have come to live in England, or pieces that have been brought back by people who have lived, worked or travelled in Burma. These textiles are wrapped in their owners' personal memories and stories of Burma, and the Museum collects these histories with the textiles.

The projects expand the scope of the original collection, and introduce the stories of people whose lives, like that of Green, form part of the connection between Burma and Britain. Some of the textiles are very different to those collected by Green, and have been collected or kept for different reasons. Eleanor Gaudoin (Sao Nang Sum Pu) and Sao Hkam Hip Hpa, for example, both own textiles that they have inherited from members of their family who governed part of the Shan State during the period that Green was in Burma. Today, they both live in England. They have personal recollections of and ties with Green and his family, and their stories, photographs and information about their textiles have made significant additions to the Green archive (See chapter 6.2).

Fig.2.xxiv right

'Hkahku girl weaving.'

Photograph by James Henry Green, c.1926.
'The warp beam is generally slightly above
the level of the breast beam and in this way
differs from the Nmao Valley and Kachin
loom. A simple form of frame heddle is
occasionally used and the shuttle is often
attached to the centre of the sword. In these
particulars it also differs from the Kachin
loom.' During the 2001–02 project, Green's
photographs and observations from the
1920s were shared with weavers in the
Kachin State.
Royal Pavilion, Libraries & Museums 1042

Fig.2.xxv below right

Muk Yin Haung Nan, a Lhaovo: weaver and
Lahpai Htu Raw, who made the La:cid outfits
for the Kachin textile project discuss a
booklet about the James Green Collection of
Kachin textiles presented to them when the
outfits were collected in March 2002.
Photograph by Lisa Maddigan.
Royal Pavilion, Libraries & Museums B0131

The Museum has made it a priority only to collect pieces that come with their histories. These personal stories of ownership provide invaluable contextual information for the textiles, and yet are often lost or ignored as an object passes through new owners, dealers and institutions.

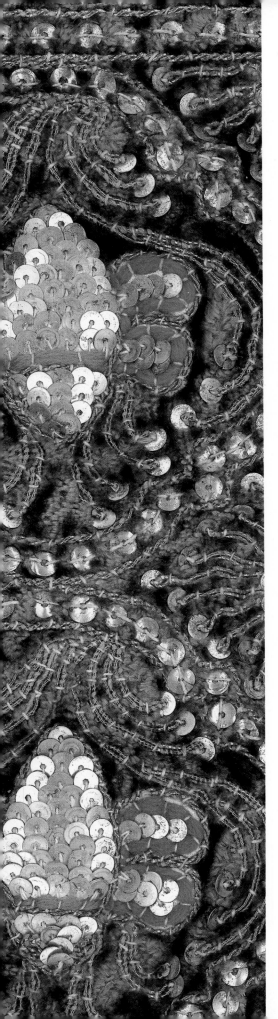

Chapter 3

Whose textiles and whose meanings?

Sandra Dudley

This chapter discusses ethnic labelling and some of the relationships between textiles/dress and identity.[1] These labels and relationships are treated uncritically in most literature specifically concerned with textiles and dress. This can be problematic. How far, for example, can we be sure that a particular textile is from a particular group? Why does it matter? What levels of 'accuracy' (if such a thing exists), are found in ascriptions of ethnic identity to textiles by collectors and museums? To what degree are the boundaries between the groups and categories blurred, and how far do they, and 'traditions', change over time?[2]

'Identity' and the urge to label

'Identity' is a problematic term, a catch-all for the political, ethnic, national, cultural, socio-economic, territorial and gender frameworks that give structure and meaning to people's lives. It is changeable and gets manipulated, by 'insiders' and 'outsiders' (the latter including collectors and anthropologists, for example) alike.[3] 'Ethnic identity' and 'ethnicity' are aspects of identity that are socially constructed categories through which people think in terms of 'us' and 'them'. How one defines a particular ethnic identity, however, depends on one's perspective,

Detail: hood. Palaung, Shan State,
late 19th century. See Fig.3.xi.

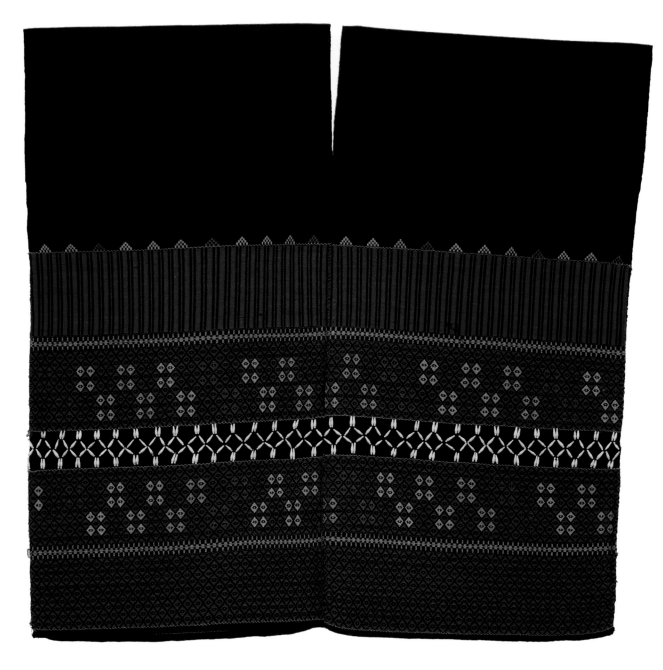

whom one asks, why one cares, and how far one values the ways in which the people concerned define themselves. Furthermore, contemporary social and political factors mean that ethnic groups in Burma, as elsewhere, are increasingly familiar with the international importance of *having* and projecting an 'identity' in the first place.[4] For Karenni refugees, for example, not only their pluralistic society but nationalism, displacement, and associated increasing awareness of the international political importance of having an 'identity' make the articulation and reformation of Karenni-ness among some sectors of their society a highly self-conscious and deliberate endeavour.[5]

Fig.3.ii above

'Sagaw [Sgaw] girl pounding rice.'

Photograph by James Henry Green, 1920s.

Note the 'Job's tears' (grass seed) decoration

on her shirt.

Royal Pavilion, Libraries & Museums 1529

Fig.3.i left

Woman's shirt. Sgaw Karen. Woven on a

backstrap loom, in an unidentified Karen

refugee camp, and purchased for the

Museum from WEAVE (Women's Education

for Advancement and Empowerment; a

non-governmental organisation based in

Chiang Mai) by Sandra Dudley, 1997.

Embroidered and decorated with 'Job's tears'.

This traditional style Karen shirt is still worn

by some Karen women, particularly for

special occasions. However lighter and more

brightly coloured shirts, machine made

without the seeds, are more prevalent now in

the refugee camps at least.

720 mm x 685 mm.

Royal Pavilion, Libraries & Museums

WA508078

From colonial times onwards, a large proportion of anthropological and other work on Burma and beyond has been preoccupied with defining ethnic categories and tracing ethnohistory in a region characterised by a staggering ethnic plurality.[6] Much literature is focused on how one can tell who belongs to what group, an approach in which identities are seen as fixed categories clearly associated with different forms of textiles and dress. Indeed, textiles and dress, with language, have often become *the* means by which outsiders distinguish and classify different groups. In practice, however, three factors – category boundaries are often blurred, 'traditions' change over time, and definitions of both are subjective – mean that it is not easy to say that wearing costume 'y' is absolutely typical of people belonging to group 'x'. What appears to be objective explanation depends upon where and when one stands, and historical and ethnological 'facts' are in reality subjective and changeable. For this reason, I argue that what matters is not the 'facts' *per se*, but the ways in which real people make, see and use them.

Perceptions amongst Burma's ethnic groups of the relationships between themselves and other ethnic groups are complex, and often intimately bound up with nationalism and other political ideologies, as well as influenced by colonial, missionary, and scholastic definitions of ethnicities.[7] External perspectives often continue either to ignore self-descriptions (or lack of) in their classifications, or to generalise from only a few.[8] In these historical and external classifications, ethno-linguistic criteria and cultural factors, especially those concerning textiles and dress, seem to be most significant. Yet in practice, while analytically these classifications may be recognised as contentious and far from the simple categories they are usually thought to be, at the same time, insiders and outsiders *do* need some way of identifying and distinguishing different ethnic groups.

In working with museum collections, for example, outsiders particularly want a way of identifying the most likely ethnic source of a specific object. Acknowledging the subjectivity of identity constructions is all very well, but in practice, we need somehow to reconcile this with the need to know something of the origin and subsequent history of a specific artefact. This methodological paradox is especially pointed in the case of textiles and other elements of dress and ornament, as it is costume that has so often been used to demarcate and perpetuate ethnic stereotypes, both in past literature[9] and in the present political climate. It remains impossible to resist forcing textiles (and ultimately people) into pigeonholes and at the same time to document textiles as informatively as possible.

Moreover, there is an ethical as well as a methodological paradox. While on the one hand it is problematic to force textiles and people into fixed categories with often arbitrary boundaries, *not* attributing labels on the grounds of political correctness or out of fear of being wrong, could imply 'non-recognition and non-concern for the people in question, for their craft traditions, artistic talents, past material culture, etc.'[10]

Fig.3.iii

'Three old Nung women, hair in front.'
'The Mother's meeting. "I don't just know
what is coming over the younger generation."
"Just look at those girls actually wearing
jackets." "Thank goodness we never did that
sort of thing when we were girls." Old Nung
women from near the source of the
Irrawaddy.' Photograph by James Henry
Green, caption from the Rangoon Gazette
Pictorial Supplement, 1931.
Many of the images in the Green Collection
suggest the process of change and
adaptation that 'traditional' costume was
perceived to be undergoing in the 1920s.
Here, three women are seen wearing the
plain hemp clothes that Green believed
comprised the 'traditional' Nung
women's costume.
Royal Pavilion, Libraries & Museums 0050

Change over time

There is, then, usually no option but to pigeonhole textiles while simultaneously recognising not only that the labels applied (by 'insiders' as well as 'outsiders') are subjective and often politically problematic, but also that they change over time as well as according to whom one asks. In itself, this can be an interesting and revealing way in which to research objects. For example, while conducting field research in Karenni refugee camps in Thailand in 1998, I showed Burmese Karen and Karenni friends photographs of Karen textiles I had examined in museum collections in Great Britain and North America. The textiles concerned were primarily indigo dyed tunics, heavily decorated with embroidery and 'Job's tears' stitched onto the garment in geometric patterns (Fig.3.i). They had all been collected from at least 100 years ago, and were all described in their museum documentation as being Burmese Karen from Karen State. Those friends to whom

Fig.3.iv above

High school students dancing for dïy-küw, the second most important traditional festival of the Karenni year, Karenni Refugee Camp 5, 1996. The students and musicians went round the camp from one end to the other, dancing in front of different houses in order to bring good fortune to them for the forthcoming year. The young women are wearing 'national Karenni' dress, comprising a red, warp-striped skirtcloth and cloak, a blouse, and a sash. The young men mostly wear Shan-style trousers with white shirts and pink headcloths.
Photograph by Sandra Dudley.

Fig.3.v top right

High school students dancing for dïy-küw, Karenni Refugee Camp 5, 1996. Photograph shows back of the women's costume. The actions of the dance represent the year's various activities (agricultural, cooking, weaving, etc.).
Photograph by Sandra Dudley.

Fig.3.vi right

Recently arrived, traditionally dressed Kayah refugee women and children, at a standpipe, Karenni Refugee Camp 2, Thailand, 1996. The picture shows clearly the back of the traditional Kayah headcloth – compare with the cloaks in Fig.3.v.
Photograph by Richard Than Tha.

I showed the photographs were mostly women, all of whom were prolific weavers and highly knowledgeable about textiles of various ethnic groups and areas. They could not accept, however, that these tunics could be Burmese Karen: they all insisted that the degree of seed decoration meant that the garments must have been made by Thai Karen instead. I, meanwhile, remained convinced that in most if not all cases the textiles were indeed made and collected in Burma and not Thailand: their collection history (most often they were collected by missionaries or colonial officers), the precise nature of some of the provenancing, and the corroboration in the form of archive photographs of Burmese Karen wearing such garments (Fig.3.ii), all seemed irrefutable. And yet for many Burmese Karen today, on appearance alone the garments must be Thai Karen. This demonstrates not only the potentially problematic nature of museum and other outsider identifications, but also the degree to which the meanings and presumed origins of textiles can change over time. This change could be an alteration in aesthetics and techniques within one location, or a real human shift: in the Karen

case as in many others, for example, for a variety of economic and political reasons there has been ongoing migration south and eastwards up to the present day. Possibly those groups who made the sorts of tunics of which I showed my informants photographs *are* now mostly to be found either on the Thai side of the border and/or so much further south in Burma that the technique was not one that my more northerly Karen friends associated with their Burmese Karen kin.

'Tradition'

Like many others of his day and afterwards, Green was worried about the dying out of 'tradition', and saw himself as recording traditional ways of life before they disappeared forever.[11] For Green and his ilk, this notion of 'tradition' is often symbolised by dress, and most especially by female dress (Fig.3.iii). Male dress shows a greater variety, with men wearing shorts, skirtcloths or trousers, while still today women dress far more 'traditionally', whatever that may mean to different people. Indeed, women seem 'charged more than men with upholding a group's culture and identity'.[12] Furthermore, the significance of women's dress in particular lies not only in its ability to signal ethnic similarity and distinction, but also in the preservation of prevailing morality. Female clothing is embedded in processes by which those with most power in determining political and communal agendas seek both to uphold morality and, in many cases, to strengthen national or other identities.[13]

Ideas about Kachin-ness or Karenni-ness or whatever are thus frequently expressed through appropriate clothes, particularly women's clothes, worn especially on religious, national and traditional occasions. But what does it actually mean for something to be considered 'traditional' and authentically characteristic of a particular ethnic identity? 'Traditional', 'national' Karenni dress as worn by women in the Karenni refugee camps in Thailand, for example (Fig.3.iv and Fig.3.v), is a 'tradition' invented for political purposes,[14] to be worn by female members of all the Karenni ethnic groups (Paku Karen, Kayan, Kayah, Kayaw, etc.) on ceremonial occasions. In the colouring and warp stripe patterning of the skirtcloth and cloak, it is clearly related to the traditional costume worn by recently arrived Kayah women refugees from remote Kayah villages (Fig.3.v, Fig.3.vi and Fig.3.vii). There are two important differences to the wider, 'national' form of dress, however. Firstly, it does not expose the amounts of female flesh that the traditional Kayah version does. Secondly, it is considered 'national Karenni', not Kayah, dress not only by Kayah members of the longer-staying refugee population but by all that population's other members too.

This form of dress was developed by members of the growing national movement after 1948, and is a transformation of 'tradition' that includes and transforms elements of traditional Kayah dress.[15] Like other promulgations of 'tradition', it 'actively appropriates aspects of perceived modernity in

reconstruction of indigenous identity'.[16] In this case, the appropriated 'aspects of perceived modernity' concern propriety, with women becoming more covered up. Furthermore, concurrently with ideas about dress, notions of proper feminine behaviour are also transformed. For example, young, unmarried, traditional Kayah girls joke about their breastcloth, (which usually only covers one breast), saying their boyfriends can have the exposed breast now, but they have to wait until marriage to get their hands on the other one. Such sexual banter is in sharp contrast to the self-consciously demure way in which most other refugee Karenni girls behave. Increasing nationalism, here accompanied by increasing Christianity, seems also to imply growing conservatism, especially with respect to women and their sexuality. In this case, it is female dress that undergoes the most obvious conservative transformation.

It has been suggested that an engagement with modernity can frequently imply a devaluation of local culture.[17] In the case of traditional Kayah female dress, an essentially female signification and reinforcement of cultural identity has in its untransmuted, traditional form, been devalued and ultimately rejected by the mainly male groups that dominate contemporary ideas of Karenni-ness. As a result, *transformation* of traditional female dress has come to represent to many Karenni *continuation* of a body of tradition that identifies Karenni people as having a distinct and glorious history *and* emergence as a modern, Christian, educated and united people.

This continuation and transformation of tradition is, like the dynamics surrounding most 'traditional' and 'national' costumes, part of a set of processes aimed at ensuring that Karenni identity remains Karenni, and at keeping Karenni people clearly distinct from others. 'Tradition' is always and everywhere dynamic:

Fig.3.ix above

Tunic. Palaung, Shan State, late 19th century. T-shaped green silk velvet jacket, with V-front and popstud rear neck opening. Red wool cloth binding at neck, with embroidery, and panel of embroidery on the front above a rectangle of red wool. 1055 mm x 505 mm. Royal Pavilion, Libraries & Museums WA508619.2

outsiders, especially when, for example, looking at museum objects, often see 'traditional' textiles as representative of a time when things were fixed and unchanging, but in fact styles, techniques, and the meanings attached by insiders to textiles and other objects are always being added to, subtracted from, and modified in other ways.[18]

We are sometimes advised to discern the difference between 'genuine' traditions and 'invented' ones, but perhaps this is unhelpful. In reality, people live in a continuum of time and what matters to them is what they *call* 'traditional', not necessarily how 'authentic' this tradition actually is. And in any case how can we be sure that one tradition is 'genuine' and another 'invented'? To label traditions in this way is often both arbitrary and irrelevant to the lives of those concerned, however much it may seem to make sense from an art historical or museological perspective. Perhaps it is more helpful instead to see 'tradition' as being like a language that is continually re-articulated 'within a modern dialogue rather than [being] a fossil from the past'.[19] A 'tradition', in other words, is what is seen as 'traditional' by those who claim ownership of it; i.e. it is not what is unchanging but what is 'represented as unchanging'.[20]

Political and other aspects of labelling

In current contexts, both self-labelling and labelling by others, including that done through and by dress and textiles, is highly political. Amongst Karenni refugees, for example, to emphasise pan-Karenni-ness or even pan-Karen-ness, and self-consciously to invent 'traditional', 'national' dress, is to insist that the extent of

Fig.3.xi

Hood. Palaung, Shan State, late 19th century. Appliqué comprises layered strips of scarlet, plain weave brushed wool, with sections of pale pink, Chinese silk brocade with flower motif, olive green silk velvet-pile fabric, with embroidered stitching, and ornate kalaga style raised sequin-pattern in silver sequins, metal thread and glass and pearlised beads. Sewn into a long hood shape, on backing of undyed, handspun cotton.
1320 mm x 440 mm.
Royal Pavilion, Libraries & Museums
WA508619.1

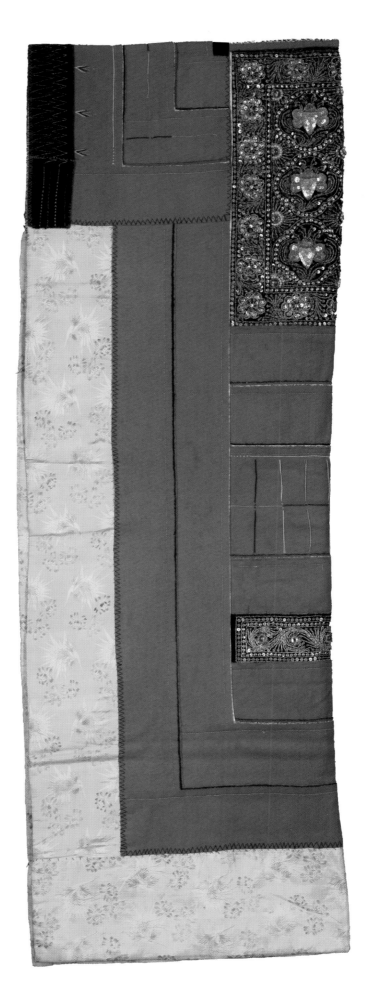

Fig.3.xii

Hat for unmarried woman. Palaung, Kalaw, Shan State, purchased in 1996. Black quilted velvet cap, lined with white cotton, decorated with sequins, embroidery and pompoms. Royal Pavilion, Libraries & Museums WA507471

diversity within the Karenni population be minimised. It is largely a reaction against what are perceived by many non-Burman ethnic groups as Burmese government tendencies to emphasise ethnic diversity and thus fracture the opposition. Some Palaung, for example, claim that the division of their people by others into 'Shwe [Golden] Palaung' and 'Ngwe [Silver] Palaung' and the separate representation and slightly different dress of each in official cultural events, constitute an attempt by the Burmese to divide a pan-Palaung community and sense of purpose (Fig.3.viii to Fig.3.xii)).[21] Many Pa-O interpret their classification by others into Black and White Pa-O similarly.[22] Such situations are complex, and while Rangoon may indeed benefit from ethnic divisions, sometimes the revisionism may also be on the part of the ethnic groups themselves. Non-nationally conscious members of some ethnic groups *do* sometimes think of other, related, neighbouring groups as considerably different, so that amongst the Karenni, for example, many Kayah see the Kayan as very different from themselves, and Kayah from other areas may perceive other Kayah as also quite distinct.[23] Ideas of a pan-Karenni-ness or pan-Karen-ness or pan-Palaung-ness or pan-whatever, and of a 'national' dress for that pan-ethnicity, are relatively new. That is not to say, however, that they are invalid.

While members of Karenni groups, for example, do regularly discuss and engage with issues of ethnicity, including in the context of textiles and dress, they do so primarily in ways that focus on differences, similarities and dynamic relationships between groups and subgroups. For outsiders on the other hand, be they local, Thai, European or other, the primary focus is generally in trying to understand, for example, Karenni subgroups as parts of a coherent, logical whole. When doing my fieldwork, I lost count of the number of times outsiders, especially those from Europe and North America, would ask not only how the various Karenni groups 'fitted together', but also what characterised the 'traditional dress' of each group. They wanted a neat model of ethno-linguistic categories showing who is a subgroup of whom, together with diagnostic criteria based on each group's dress. Scott's words are still pertinent, and apply more generally:

> All the later authorities are convinced that the Karens have suffered from over-classification. The early missionaries set themselves to the work with more zeal than discrimination ... Their clans read like a table of fashion plates or a history of tartans. The only visible distinction between one clan and another was the dress worn ... This is catching, but it is not scientific or satisfactory.
> Scott 1911: 120

What follows in chapter 4 and beyond, should, on the one hand, be seen in the context of the linguistic and cultural categories into which Burma's various ethnic groups do theoretically fit, and with the understanding that there is an ethical consideration in crediting originating communities with the beautiful textiles they have produced. But on the other hand, it should also be read with the awareness that neat, universally comprehensible, fixed ethnological categories are both impossible to construct and often irrelevant to large numbers of the people to whom they are supposed to refer. Furthermore, categories and traditions are always in flux.

Chapter 4
Textile traditions of Burma: a brief overview

4.1 Akha textiles

Mika Toyota

The fabric used in Akha clothing is closely woven cotton, dyed blue-black. Making textiles is primarily women's work. Traditionally, the Akha grew their own cotton and out of the raw substance made 'turfs' about 20 cm long. This was put into small bamboo containers, fastened to the belt, and the cotton was then drawn out to be spun. Akha girls learned to spin when they were as young as six or seven years. Akha women would spin thread even while walking to the fields.

Weaving is a dry season activity. The loom is set up after harvesting in late November. The Akha loom consists of a simple scaffold-type frame fitted to uprights in the ground, with the operator standing in the middle working a foot treadle. These rudimentary looms can be easily assembled and dismantled (Fig.4.1.i). The resultant close textured cloth, about 20 cm wide, is dyed with the leaves of *Polygonum tinctorium*, (*myang* in Akha), a low-lying shrub that differs from *Indigofera tinctoria*, the best known source of indigo dye.[1] Akha cloth requires up to 30 days of daily dipping and drying in order to produce the characteristic, deep blue-black hue.

Detail: jacket. Lomi Akha, Kengtung, Shan State. See Fig.4.1.iv.

Fig.4.1.i above

'Kaw [Akha] woman weaving.'
Scaffold-type frame loom, fitted to uprights in
the ground, and worked using a foot treadle.
Photograph by James Henry Green, 1920s.
Royal Pavilion, Libraries & Museums 1516

Fig.4.1.iii right

Headdress. Lomi Akha, made in Sungsak
village, near Kengtung, Shan State, c.1960.
Flat headdress on woven cotton base,
decorated with silver alloy medallions beaten
from coins, with seeds and beads. Worn by
married Akha women.
Royal Pavilion, Libraries & Museums
WA507480

Fig.4.1.ii *above*

'Kaw [Akha] girl standing.'

Photograph by James Henry Green, 1920s.

Royal Pavilion, Libraries & Museums P0091

Fig.4.1.v *top right*

Headdress. Phami Akha, purchased in
Xishuang Bana, Yunnan, southwest China,
in 1995. Helmet-shaped headdress,
encrusted with buttons beaten from silver
alloy, coins, beads and insects. This style is
worn primarily by the Maw Po clan in
Thailand, Burma and China.

Royal Pavilion, Libraries & Museums
WA507621

Fig.4.1.iv *right*

Jacket. Lomi Akha, made in Sungsak village,
near Kengtung, Shan State. Indigo dyed cotton
jacket made of four pieces, appliquéd and
embroidered in polychrome using repeating,
contrasting diamonds and triangle motifs.
Decorated with seeds and 'Job's tears', and
tassels made of beads and cotton.
460 mm x 680 mm.

Royal Pavilion, Libraries & Museums
WA507482

Although Akha weaving is restricted to a plain weave and the dye to a single blue-black colour, their costume is still one of the most spectacular outfits in the hills. The basic clothing of an Akha woman consists of a headdress, a jacket worn over a halter-like garment, a short skirt, a sash with decorated ends, leggings and a shoulder bag (Fig.4.1.ii). Dress is so distinctive that Paul and Elaine Lewis, American Baptist missionaries, who worked amongst Akha from 1947 to 1966 in Burma's Kengtung area, used it to differentiate the Akha into three subgroups.[2] The first style, a pointed headdress worn by *A jaw* Akha in Burma resembles that of *Ulo* Akha in Thailand. *Ulo* Akha jackets are embroidered with rows of small running stitch lines and cross-stitch in zigzags and other motifs (Fig.4.1.ii). The second style is a flat headdress worn by *Lomi* Akha (Fig.4.1.iii) with a jacket decorated with appliquéd rows of contrasting diamonds and triangles (Fig.4.1.iv). The third style, shaped like a helmet and encrusted with silver buttons, coins and beads, is worn by *Phami* Akha (Fig.4.1.v), primarily by the Mang Po clan in Thailand, Burma and China.

4.2 Burman textiles

Sylvia Fraser-Lu

The Burmans have long been noted for their love of boldly patterned, brightly coloured clothing made from home-grown cotton, and imported Chinese silk. During the Konbaung period (1752–1885), traditional women's dress comprised the *htamein*, a rectangular, wrap-around ankle-length skirt secured under the arms or around the waist (Fig.4.2.i). The upper band of plain fabric was sewn to a wider central section featuring the main design elements, and the *htamein* terminated in a lighter coloured, horizontally striped section, with the excess gathered in a train at the back. The *htamein* opened in the front, and was usually worn with a breastcloth and a neat-fitting, light-coloured tailored jacket (*eingyi*) of muslin or quilted cotton. A shawl (*pawa*) might be added for wearing in public.

The Burman male was equally resplendent in a voluminous garment, the *pahso* (Fig.4.2.ii). This rectangle of cloth measuring approximately 4000 mm by 1500 mm was made from two identical lengths sewn together. It could be worn either as a sarong with the excess falling in folds in front or draped over one shoulder, or, when worn while working, as a pair of breeches formed by passing one of end of the cloth through the legs and securing it at the waist. *Eingyi* were also worn by men on formal occasions. A colourful silk or muslin headcloth folded in various ways, depending on the age of the wearer, completed the outfit along with the open sandals worn by both sexes.

Such basic garments were worn by all classes. Social distinctions were marked by the fabric quality, design intricacy and the use of silk rather than by the garment's style and cut. Stripes and plaids in both cotton and silk were widely worn by all. The brightest and most boldly patterned items were preferred by the young, while subdued colours and smaller designs were the province of the elderly. Upper class men often wore knee-length semi-diaphanous jackets on formal occasions. Fabrics embellished with metallic threads were limited by sumptuary laws to royalty, high officials and tributary princes, who appeared at court on formal occasions weighted down by heavy gold and sequin embroidered coat-like costumes crowned by soaring headdresses.

Detail: skirtcloth (htamein). Burman,
Amarapura, 20th century. See Fig.4.2.iii.

Fig.4.2.i

A young Burman woman in a luntaya acheik patterned htamein, breastcloth and eingyi jacket. Photographed c.1900 in Rangoon, by P. Klier.

The most sought after fabric for *htamein* and *pahso* was *luntaya acheik*. This expensive, horizontally patterned silk cloth was – and is – woven in the Amarapura area on a traditional Thai-Burmese loom in an interlocking tapestry weave by pairs of girls who painstakingly manipulate 100–200 small shuttles back and forth in turn through a warp of over 1,500 threads. The distinctive wave like cable designs sometimes include floral appendages and are often in striking *trompe l'oeil* colour combinations (Fig.4.2.iii, Fig.4.2.iv). The Burmans credit the introduction of the tapestry weaving technique to captive weavers from Manipur in the late eighteenth century.[1] So highly prized was *luntaya acheik* that its patterns offered inspiration to textile producers in other parts of Burma. Weavers in Arakan on the west coast and Gangaw in central Burma began to integrate *acheik* elements

Fig.4.2.ii

A dapper young Burman man in a patterned pahso, fur-lined eingyi jacket, and headcloth. Photographed c.1900 in Rangoon, by P. Klier.

into their traditional supplementary weft-patterned fabrics, as did the weavers of *ikat* at Inle Lake, Kyi-thei near Prome and Thabyei Auk in the Mandalay area (Fig.4.2.iv).

While *luntaya acheik* continues to be the Burman national fabric, lifestyle changes in colonial times led to the abandonment of the traditional *htamein* and *pahso* in favour of the ubiquitious *longyi,* a tubular sarong (c. 1000 mm × 1800 mm) worn differently by each sex. Men have also largely forsaken their headcloths for ready-made *gaung baung* turbans of light coloured, stiffened muslin.

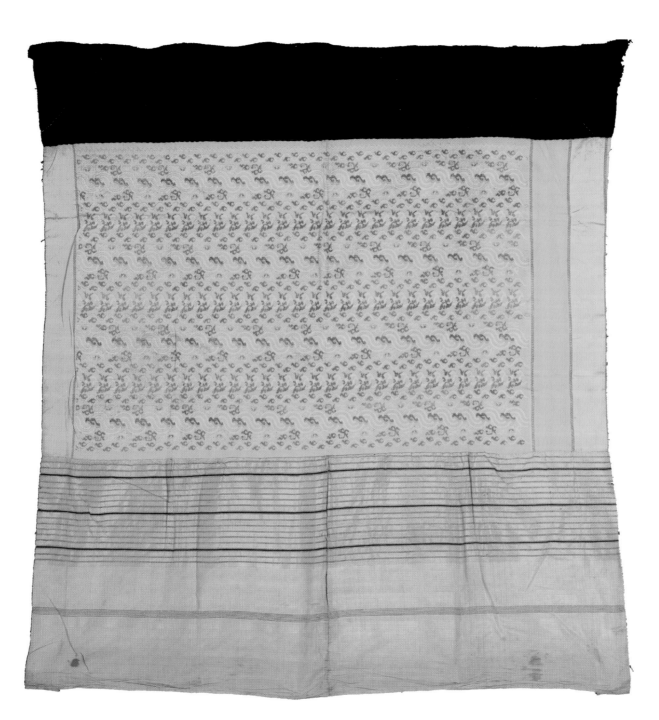

Fig.4.2.iii

Skirtcloth (htamein). Burman, Amarapura,
20th century. Woman's luntaya acheik
patterned htamein. Interlocking tapestry
weave made from chemically dyed Chinese
silk. Fabric is formed into a tube, backed with
fine undyed cotton. 1180 mm x 1055 mm.
Royal Pavilion, Libraries & Museums
WA508247

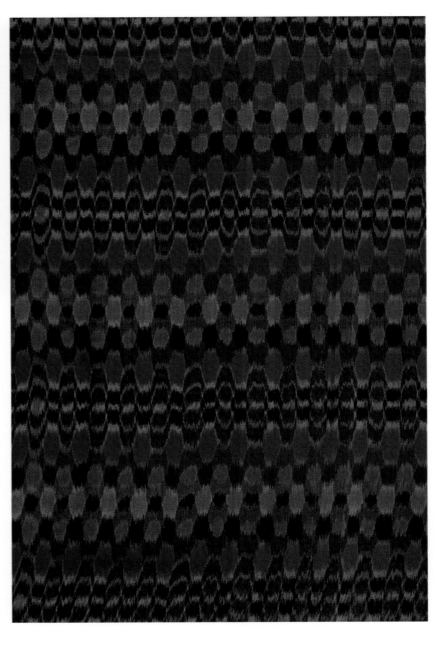

Fig.4.2.v *above*

100 shuttle loom, Amarapura, 1996. This traditional Thai-Burmese loom is worked by pairs of girls to produce the highly sought after interlocking tapestry weave, luntaya acheik. 100 to 200 small shuttles are painstakingly worked back and forth in turn through a warp of over 1,500 threads. Photograph by Elizabeth Dell.

Fig.4.2.iv. *right*

Detail of skirtcloth (longyi), Burman, Thabyei Auk village, Mandalay Division, mid 1990s. Woman's longyi made from chemically dyed cotton, weft ikat design inspired by luntaya acheik designs. 950 mm x 1150 mm. Royal Pavilion, Libraries & Museums WA507411

The Burmans have not, however, forsaken their sacred obligation to provide the Buddhist monkhood with daily necessities. The faithful continue to supply saffron robes, which, with the exception of those produced from lotus stem fibre, are now machine-made and store-purchased rather than woven and dyed at home. Crocheted bowl holders continue to be made as acts of merit by some devotees. Closely patterned ribbons called *sazigyo*, woven on a tablet loom and used to bind sacred texts within their bamboo stiffened cloth covers, ceased to be made in the 1970s.

4.3 Chin textiles

John Barker

The Chin (or Zo) comprise some 70 groups[1] having linguistic affiliations with neighbouring Nagas and, more distantly, Burmans.[2] In numerous groups, women skillfully used backstrap looms to weave distinctively patterned textiles for ceremonial and everyday use. In a few isolated areas, traditional textile manufacture and use continue today. While 'traditions' are always fluid, for most Chin the cultural, economic and political changes of the last century have had particular impact on both the weaving and wearing of textiles. As elsewhere, 'traditional' weaving continues to change or even cease as weavers die without passing on their skills. The small number of examples that can be discussed here illustrates something of the extraordinary diversity and artistry of Chin textiles.

In the northern and central regions of Chin State, several groups still weave striking, patterned red silk textiles; today's version is more loosely woven than earlier examples. These include a cloth, skirtcloth, tunic (Fig.4.3.i, Fig.6.1.ii, Fig.6.1.iii), and shawl (*puan lep*). They typically contain bands with series of small, discrete diamond motifs that stand out in vibrant contrast to the ground weave. These silk styles are reportedly a late nineteenth century Zotung-Zophei Chin innovation that gradually spread to the Haka, Zahau, Lautu and Mara.[3] Subtle colour or design variations are associated with different groups. For example, the diamond patterning of the twill-weave band on the man's cloth is distinctly Zahau (Fig.4.3.i). An earlier tradition of these groups features weft-faced cloths of hand spun, indigo-dyed cotton (Fig.4.3.ii). These are subtly patterned with geometric forms, some of which have symbolic meanings.[4] Such cloths were reserved for higher status men and their families. Other northern groups, including the Ngawn, Taisun, Lushai, Zanniat, Sim and Thado, also produced finely patterned weavings and in some cases today produce modern versions for use or sale.

Detail: woman's skirtcloth (hnitial). Haka, central Chin State. See Fig.6.1.ii, page 145.

Fig.4.3.i

Man's cloth (cawng nak). Zahau, northern
Chin State. Silk; warp-faced tabby ground, twill
weave, discontinuous supplementary weft
patterning. 2120 mm x 1260 mm.
Hollander collection

Fig.4.3.ii

Man's cloth (cheulopang). Mara Chin, central
Chin State. Cotton, silk; weft-faced tabby
ground with discontinuous supplementary
weft patterning. 2060 mm x 1270 mm.
Hollander collection

Fig.4.3.iv *above*

Breastcover (akhin). Khami, northwest
Rakhaing State. Cotton, silk; warp-faced tabby
ground with multiple supplementary weft
weaves. 700 mm x 320 mm.
Hollander collection

Several southern Chin groups employed one or more densely woven, supplementary weft techniques over warp-faced ground weaves, to produce cloths intricately patterned on one side. Ingenious variations in the woven structure create complex, textured effects. In northwest Arakan (Rakhaing) State, Khami and Khumi weavings embody these features. The man's loincloth and woman's breastcover (Fig.4.3.iii) and (Fig.4.3.iv) have added yarns of varying colour and thickness, producing rich visual effects. Such loincloths were a traditional gift from wife to husband and took nearly a year to weave.[5] To the west, other Khami wove the same types but with very different compositions (Fig.4.3.v, Fig.4.3.vi). The Khami Arang examples display a lively repeat motif (Fig.6.1.v, Fig.6.1.vi). Neighbouring Khumi also wove vibrantly patterned textiles such as beaded skirts *(neina)* and breastcovers *(ne kouk)*. Nearby Mro peoples, too, are known for their finely patterned weavings. In some areas, simplified versions of all these types are still produced today.

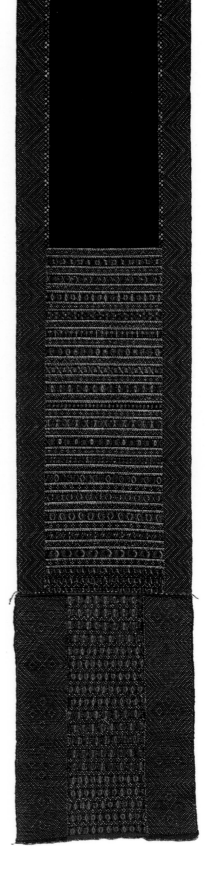

Fig.4.3.iii *right*

Detail: man's loincloth (paderi). Khami,
northwest Rakhaing State. Cotton, silk, glass
beads, plastic beads; warp-faced tabby
ground with multiple supplementary weft
weaves. 4280 mm x 170 mm.

Hollander collection

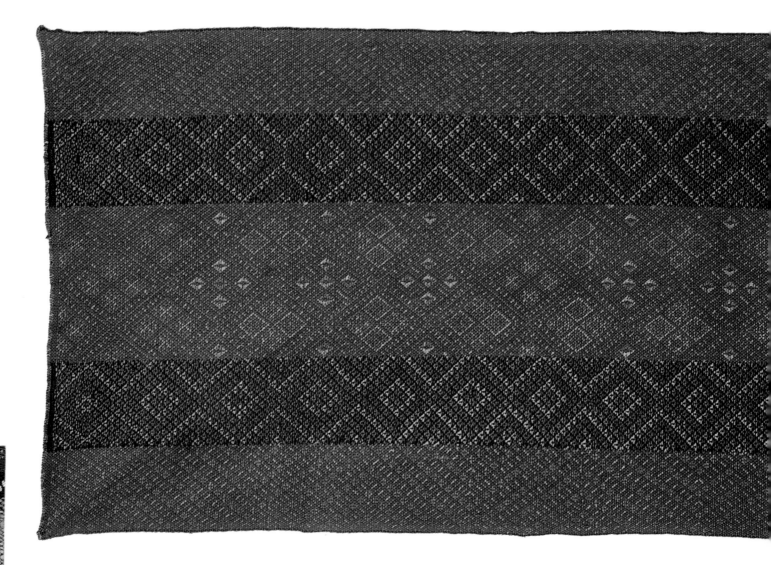

Fig.4.3.vi above
*Breastcover (akhin). Khami, Buthidaung
township, northwest Rakhaing State.
Cotton, silk; warp-faced tabby ground with
supplementary weft patterning (inlay).
700 mm x 340 mm.
Hollander collection*

To the southeast, Sungtu weavers still produce long tunics ornamented with beads, shells and a wide band of magenta diamond patterning (Fig.4.3.vii). Along the Lemro river, Laytu women created ornate, beaded short tunics (Fig.4.3.viii, Fig.4.3.ix); today a much simpler, 'everyday' variant is still produced. Along the Dalet river, Lauktu women wear long tunics *(chan)*; only a few elderly Lauktu still have the skills needed to weave fine-patterned silk headcloths (Fig.6.1.vii).

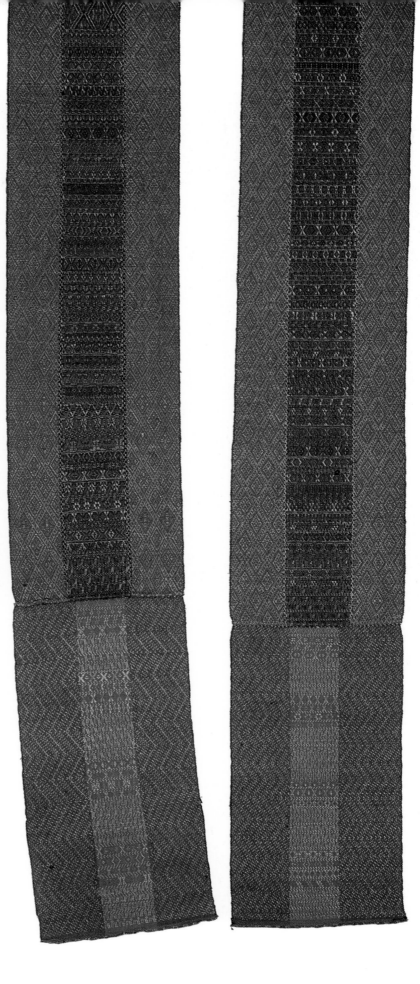

Fig.4.3.v *right*

Detail: man's loincloth (paderi). Khami,
Buthidaung township, northwest Rakhaing
State. Cotton; warp-faced tabby ground with
multiple supplementary weft weaves.
4580 mm x 170 mm.
Hollander collection

Fig.4.3.vii

*Woman's long tunic (khreng tan). Sungtu,
northwest Rakhaing State. Cotton, ?silk, glass
beads, buttons; warp-faced tabby ground with
supplementary weft patterning (inlay),
embroidery. 900 mm x 820 mm.
Hollander collection*

Fig.4.3.viii *right*

Woman's or man's short tunic (khran in).
Laytu, Myebon township, northwest Rakhaing
State. Cotton, glass beads, cowrie shells;
warp-faced tabby ground with supplementary
weft patterning (inlay). 480 mm x 460 mm.
Hollander collection

Fig.4.3.ix *below right*

Woman's short tunic (khran hain). Laytu
(northern), Minbya township, northwest
Rakhaing State. Cotton, ?silk, buttons, metallic
sequins; warp-faced tabby ground with
multiple supplementary weft weaves.
380 mm x 410 mm.
Hollander collection

4.4 Kachin textiles

Lisa Maddigan

In the 1920s, James Green recognised that dress was one way of categorising the groups of people that he came across in the Kachin hills of northern Burma. For special occasions such as festivals, weddings and funerals, Kachin people wear richly decorated outfits that distinguish them as being part of a particular Kachin group. These groupings were originally loosely based on geographical regions of what is today Kachin State. Communities still live in these areas, although many of the groups have been dispersed and urban centres like Myitkyina have become home to people from all of the different Kachin groups. Today, what is described in Myitkyina as 'traditional dress' continues to play a significant role in defining and displaying Kachin identity, and is still worn for special occasions and cultural events. The designs used and the group definitions associated with particular styles are not fixed and change over time. However, Kachin traditional dress continues to incorporate elements of the styles and techniques that Green observed in the 1920s.

The traditional style outfits currently associated with different Kachin groups are diverse in form and in use of materials, techniques and designs. Within this, the style associated with the most dominant Kachin group, the Jinghpaw Manmaw, is often singled out to represent Kachin traditional dress both inside and outside Kachin State (Fig.4.4.i). The man's outfit usually consists of black, Shan-style trousers, worn with a white shirt, a plain white, tailored, Mao-style jacket, and a yellow silk turban, all purchased in the market place. A red bag with hand woven supplementary weft designs and silver decorations is worn with a silver sword, both of which would have been presented to the wearer at his marriage. The woman's outfit consists of a wrap-around, calf-length skirtcloth secured with a cotton belt, and worn with woven leggings and a headdress. The highest quality skirtcloths are woven by hand on a backstrap loom and can take months

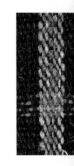

Detail: cloth, Kachin Jinghpaw, northern Kachin State and Hukawng valley, collected in the 1920s. This type of cloth is used as a ritual textile in many ways, for dowries or funeral flags, for example.
Royal Pavilion, Libraries & Museums
G000221

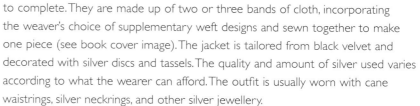

to complete. They are made up of two or three bands of cloth, incorporating the weaver's choice of supplementary weft designs and sewn together to make one piece (see book cover image). The jacket is tailored from black velvet and decorated with silver discs and tassels. The quality and amount of silver used varies according to what the wearer can afford. The outfit is usually worn with cane waistrings, silver neckrings, and other silver jewellery.

Some traditional styles and techniques are shared by groups, for example the Jinghpaw Htingnai and Jinghpaw Hkahku man's dress share the same style of chequered skirtcloth, worn with a white shirt, black jacket and chequered headcloth. However, the bags carried have their own distinct styles and clearly distinguish the outfit as being either Htingnai or Hkahku (Fig.4.4.ii, Fig.4.4.iii and Fig.6.3.2.ii). The Htingnai and Hkahku women's outfits are very different from each other. The Htingnai woman's skirt is woven on a backstrap loom in three pieces, richly patterned with supplementary weft designs and sewn together into a cloth

Fig.4.4.i – Fig.4.4.iii

Models wearing traditional outfits associated with the Jinghpaw Manmaw, Hkahku and Htingnai groups. The outfits were commissioned by the Museum in 2001. Photographs taken at the Manau festival ground in Myitkyina by Htoi Awng, 2002. Royal Pavilion, Libraries & Museums B0083, B0086, B0087

tied to the body with a white cotton belt. The Hkahku woman's skirt is woven in black, purple and green silk on a different type of loom that has a backstrap and a simple frame (Fig.4.4.v). The chequered patterned silk has a thin band of supplementary weft designs woven vertically down one side of the cloth. This is considered by today's Hkahku weavers to be the most traditional style of Hkahku skirtcloth; however, contemporary skirtcloths often have patterns woven all over, which many weavers see as being more attractive (Fig.4.4.vi).

A variety of designs are used to decorate current forms of traditional Kachin textiles, some are considered essential to particular outfits while most are chosen according to the weaver's preference and ability. Traditional-style skirtcloths have a 'mother pattern' woven in supplementary weft in a vertical strip down the side of the cloth (Fig.4.4.vii). The design of the mother pattern varies between Kachin groups but carries the same associations. When a woman learning to weave has mastered the mother pattern, she is considered to be competent in all of the

Fig.4.4.iv

*Man's bag (n'hpye). Kachin Jinghpaw,
southern Kachin State and northern Shan
State, collected in 1926. Cotton bag with
polychrome supplementary weft design. Front
of bag is richly encrusted with silver disks,
beads and seeds and finished with a fringe
280 mm long of red woven cotton ribbons.
Bag length, excluding strap, 610 mm x 280
mm. Decorative cotton woven and fringed
tassel attached to the strap would probably
have been presented to the wearer by
an admirer.*

*Royal Pavilion, Libraries & Museums
G000001*

basic techniques required to weave the rest of the patterns on a skirtcloth. The other designs used frequently carry associations with particular plants, household items, or can refer to Kachin traditions and mythology. The skirtcloths are traditionally woven by hand on backstrap looms; popular designs are also produced in large quantities on mechanical looms. Many women nowadays choose to have the fabric made up into tailored skirts and blouses.

Traditional Kachin outfits can incorporate many techniques and materials. These vary with the different groups' styles of dress, and according to the amount of time and money invested in an outfit. In the documentation of the textile project commissioned by the Museum in Myitkyina in 2001, weavers made frequent references to the two main weaving techniques, which they described as *lasi maka* (discontinuous supplementary weft) and *sanat maka* (continuous supplementary weft). The use and interpretation of these two techniques varied. Sadau Roi Ji, for example, who made the Jinghpaw Manmaw group's wedding outfit used the *sanat*

Fig.4.4.vi

Skirtcloth (bu bai). Kachin Jinghpaw Hkahku,
purchased at Myitkyina market in 1998.
Cotton with polychrome supplementary weft
patterns on black and purple base. Compare
with the old style Hkahku skirtcloth collected
by Green in the 1920s (Fig.2.iv).
Royal Pavilion, Libraries & Museums
WA508282

maka technique throughout, associating this complex and more time consuming method with the highest quality and most durable textiles. Weaver Lahpai Htu Raw, on the other hand, used the *lasi maka* technique to weave the Zaiwa group woman's skirtcloth. She said that although *sanat maka* was used in the past for Zaiwa skirtcloths, today *lasi maka* is used and is a feature that distinguishes the cloth from Jinghpaw Manmaw skirts (Fig.4.4.viii). The Jinghpaw Htingnai woman's skirt, made by Maran Kai Htang, has been woven using *lasi maka*. She has hand embroidered the same style of geometric designs onto the woman's jacket, a process that she described as being more time consuming than weaving. Jackets made by Hkaw Ma Sar and associated with traditional Lisu dress, by contrast, have been cut and tailored from plain cloth. The embellishment and ornamentation is based on elaborate appliqué work, rather than weaving.

Fig.4.4.v *above*

Hkahku weaver Gwi Kai Nan, working at her loom, Myitkyina, 2002.

Photograph by Salaw Zau Ring.

Royal Pavilion, Libraries & Museums B0057

Fig.4.4.viii *right*

Skirtcloth (labu). Kachin, Zaiwa, made by Lahpai Htu Raw in Myitkyina, 2002.

Discontinuous supplementary weft (lasi maka). Wool, plastic beads.

870 mm x 1650 mm.

Royal Pavilion, Libraries & Museums WA508784

Fig.4.4.vii *above*
Weaver Lahpai Htu Raw points out the 'mother pattern' on a Zaiwa group woman's skirtcloth. She said that the same mother pattern is shared by the Zaiwa, Hkahku and Htingnai groups. Photograph taken in Myitkyina by Lisa Maddigan, 2002. Royal Pavilion, Libraries & Museums B0139

Fig.4.4.ix *right*
Woman's apron (kachyi hkyeng). Kachin Lisu, made by Hkaw Ma Sar in Myitkyina, 2001/2. Cotton, satin, wool, beads, shells, silver decorations. 955 mm x 1240 mm. Royal Pavilion, Libraries & Museums WA508731

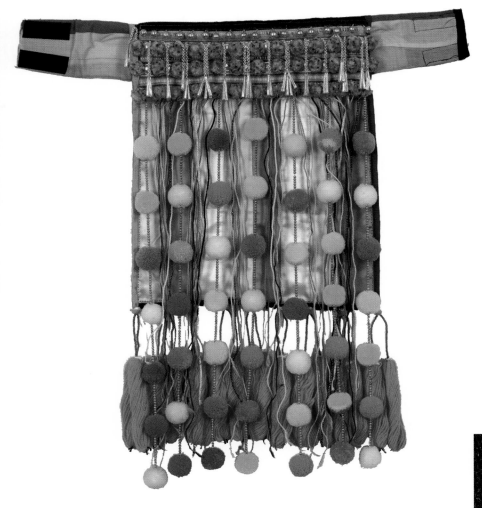

Materials for weaving and decorating vary according to outfit and the weaver's personal choice and budget. Most outfits are made from cotton and wool, but silk, hemp and synthetic fibres are also used. A variety of threads can be bought ready processed and dyed in market places. Some weavers prepare materials themselves, or might choose to do so for particular outfits. Although many weavers know how to prepare natural dyes, chemical dyes are now widely used to colour the threads. The colours red, black and yellow are dominant in many outfits.

A rich variety of embellishments are used in traditional Kachin outfits, including silver decoration, coins, seeds, orchid fibres, cowrie shells, woollen pompoms and tassels, porcelain buttons and sequins. The quality and selection of these decorations are often influenced by budget and availability, and items such as high quality silver decorations, rare coins, seeds and buttons clearly display the investment that has been made in an item of clothing.

4.5 Karenic textiles

Sandra Dudley

'Karenic' covers a number of related ethnic subgroups living mostly but not entirely in Karen State (Kayin State or Kawthoolei), Karenni State (Kayah State), the Tenasserim coast and the Irrawaddy, Sittang and Salween delta regions. Many authorities divide Karenic groups into three main cultural-linguistic divisions: Pwo Karen, who are mostly lowlanders, Sgaw Karen, found particularly in Karen State, and Bwe or Northern Karen, found particularly in Karenni State. The Pwo linguistic division includes the Pwo proper (Pho or Phlong) and the Pa-O, the latter living mainly in southern Shan State. The Sgaw include the Sgaw proper and various subgroups, including not only groups living primarily in Karen State but also the Paku Karen of southwest Karenni State. The Bwe or northern Karen include the Kayah (known in older English language literature as 'Red Karen' or Karenni), the Kayaw and closely related Manu-Manaw, the Brek, and a number of Kayan groups including the Kayan Kangkaw (Padaung), Kayan Kang-nga (Yinbaw), Gheba, Lahta, and others.

Whilst wishing to avoid labelling pitfalls, there are certain distinctions in traditional forms of dress and textile used by many of these different groups.[1] Amongst Sgaw and Pwo Karen (excluding Pa-O) groups, for example, young unmarried girls traditionally wore relatively simple and undyed shift dresses made of two long rectangular strips seamed up the sides leaving armholes and up the middle of the body leaving a gap to form a V-neck (Fig.4.5.i). Married women and often also older, unmarried girls, by contrast, adopt a coloured shirt (constructed in the same way as the shift dress), a skirtcloth sewn into a tube and worn in the usual *longyi* (sarong) way (Fig.4.5.i) and, traditionally, a long headcloth worn as a sort of turban (Fig.4.5.ii). Precise colour combinations and decorative styles utilised in the construction of this shirt, skirtcloth and headcloth vary with group, period and area. For example, many Pwo Karen married women traditionally wore all-red shirts or shirts with a white upper half and red lower half, and Pwo Karen unmarried women traditionally wore white shift dresses bearing rich red decoration. Sgaw Karen traditional dress is often said to be simpler and less

Detail: cotton headcloth, Sgaw Karen,
early 20th century. 1730 mm x 370 mm.
Royal Pavilion, Libraries & Museums
G000026

Fig.4.5.ii above

*Naw Nay Say (name changed) wearing a
Paku Karen woman's headcloth (hkopeu-oki),
Karenni Refugee Camp 5, Thailand, 1997.
Cotton, with elaborate continuous and
discontinuous supplementary weft patterning
and fringing. Such cloths are usually heirloom
objects, and would be worn by a girl for the
first time on her wedding day. After the point
in the ceremony at which marriage is
formally complete, her friends would dress
her in this 'to change her into a woman'
(personal communication, 1997).
This cloth was purchased by the author from
Naw Nay Say's aunt, and is now in the Pitt
Rivers Museum, University of Oxford.
Photograph by Sandra Dudley.*

Fig.4.5.i above right

*'Three Hill Sgaws. Two women and one man.'
Photograph by James Henry Green in the
southern Shan State, 1920s.
Royal Pavilion, Libraries & Museums P0069*

brightly coloured, but in practice this is not always so, and in any case style varies greatly with area. Women of Northern Karen groups have rather different forms of traditional dress, involving various styles of short skirtcloths, breastcloths (or tunic shirts in the case of the Kayan Kangkaw) and, often, headcloths/cloaks (Fig.4.5.iii). Kayah women and others in remote northern areas still wear their traditional style of dress, as do those Kayan Kangkaw (Padaung) women who wear neckrings (Fig.4.5.iv). Pa-O women too are perhaps particularly inclined still to wear their traditional dress – black tunic, skirtcloth, turban and, often, jacket – on a daily basis (Fig.4.5.v). These days, however, in non-remote villages many other Karenic women, married or not, are more likely to wear a T-shirt than a Karen shirt, and a market-purchased sarong printed with *batik*-style patterns. Nonetheless, more 'traditional' forms of dress are still adopted on formal occasions and, for Christians, on Sundays.

Fig.4.5.iii *above*

Recently arrived 'traditional' Kayah refugee women pounding rice, Karenni Refugee Camp 2, Thailand, 1996. The women wear red headcloths and skirtcloths (not visible) incorporating yellow warp stripes, black breastcloths, white cotton tie-belts, lacquered cotton kneerings, strings of beads, necklaces of old Indian silver rupees, and silver earplugs with pendants.

Photograph by Richard Than Tha.

Fig.4.5.iv *above right*

'Two Padaung girls and one man, standing and exchanging yeps.' Photograph by James Henry Green in the southern Shan State, 1920s. A yep was a container for holding betel nut for chewing; it was and is common practice to exchange or offer betel as a greeting when meeting friends.

Royal Pavilion, Libraries & Museums P0034

On special occasions Sgaw and Pwo Karen men wear traditional-style Karen shirts (constructed as women's shirts and shift dresses), these days usually with full-length, universal-style trousers.[2] Formerly, rather than short tunics and trousers, in many southern areas men would have worn long tunics alone, often with a headcloth. Northern Karen men, on the other hand, used to wear short pants[3] or a loincloth together with a tunic or blanket. Now on formal occasions they are more likely to wear Shan-style dress consisting of a headcloth, shirt and wide, black full-length trousers.

Fig.4.5.v *above*

'Taungthu [Pa-O] boy decorating ear of girl.'
Photograph by James Henry Green in
the 1920s.

Scott commented in 1932 that while
Taungthu [Pa-O] men tended to dress
'exactly like the Shans', the women tended to
carefully preserve their traditional patterns.
Pa-O women today are particularly likely to
wear their traditional dress on a daily basis.
The coarse black cotton tunic, skirtcloth and
jacket are defined by subtle embroidered
outlines to the hems and edges in bright
cotton thread.
Royal Pavilion, Libraries & Museums P0026

Fig.4.5.vi *above right*

Tunic (hse), Sgaw Karen, Karen State, early
20th century. Man's tunic shirt made from
two joined sections of heavy natural cotton
weave, patterned with broad red warp
striping and red continuous supplementary
weft. Weft threads are worked into long
tassels at base, armholes and neck opening.
925 mm x 760 mm.
Royal Pavilion, Libraries & Museums
G000021

Karenic weaving is traditionally and in the northern areas still most often done on a continuous warp backstrap loom,[4] usually with cotton (or, these days, polycotton), by women. Bags too are made by many groups, and a few still produce blankets. Some relatively remote Kayah and other groups still grow their own cotton and dye it with vegetable and other natural pigments. Today most women, however, buy ready-spun yarn from markets, in brighter colours pre-produced with chemical dyes. Favoured colours both today and in the past include red (Fig.4.5.vi) and indigo/black, with yellows and greens particularly favoured for decoration.[5]

Fig.4.5.vii

Tunic (hse), Sgaw Karen, Karen State, early 20th century. Woman's tunic shirt made from two joined sections of heavy, indigo dyed cotton weave, decorated with red, green and yellow continuous supplementary weft. Bottom edge, neckline and tassels in natural cotton. 765 mm x 715 mm.

Royal Pavilion, Libraries & Museums G000024

Decorative techniques used to varying degrees by most groups in the past and today include warp stripes, and in many traditional, Northern Karen cloths this is the main form of ornament. Other techniques, used in some Sgaw skirtcloths include supplementary weft, a technique that, like embroidery, is also used widely in various Pwo and Sgaw tunics (Fig.4.5.vii). Pwo and Sgaw subgroups also often utilise warp *ikat*, especially for the 'python skin' pattern on skirtcloths,[6] embellishment with Job's tears, adornment with rickrack and other braid, the addition of small areas of long fringing and sometimes pompoms to tunics, and occasionally appliqué. Paku Karen women's shirts, for example, are black, often edged around the neck and armhole with red rickrack braid or pinked felt, and decorated with embroidered, free-flowing floral motifs. Other Sgaw shirts, on the other hand, are often decorated with regularly repeated blocks, circles or other geometric designs over the lower two thirds to three quarters section.

4.6 Naga textiles

Vibha Joshi

There are over 20 Naga groups in northeast India and northwest Burma. They speak a variety of Tibeto-Burman languages and in some cases share migration myths, which reflect similarities in material culture, especially textiles. Burmese Nagas do not live under the same conditions as those in India, the latter having their own state and access to government 'development schemes' encouraging cottage industry, especially for textile production.

Nagas are known for cloth produced on backstrap looms (Fig.4.6.i). Weaving, spinning and dyeing are exclusively female. Men manufacture weaving instruments and may help warp up the thread. Backstrap woven Naga fabric is thick, due to a dense warp covering the weft. The precise thickness depends on the thread, the finest cloth being made of two-ply yarn.

Traditionally, Nagas used home-grown cotton and nettle fibres. Nettle fibres were and still are used for bedding. Cotton spinning and weaving, however, is now done in only a few villages. Even in Green's time, the Nagas had already started using yarn imported from central Burma[1] and the Assam plains.[2] Today, favourite yarns are acrylic and cashmilon, the latter a mixed wool. Metallic thread is also now used for supplementary weft motifs (Fig.4.6.ii).

Men's traditional dress comprises an apron and a kilt reaching just above the knee. Both may be decorated with cowries or 'Job's tears' (grass seeds) (Fig.4.6.iii, Fig.4.6.iv). Cloths measuring up to 1520 mm × 1020 mm are used as wraps, worn with both traditional dress and western clothing. Men wear multi-coloured sashes and belts as part of ceremonial dress. Women wear sarongs or wrap-around skirts of varying lengths, with blouses. The shawls worn by women are smaller than the men's. Sarongs are the most common form of dress, but Burmese, north Indian and western clothes are also worn by women living in townships.

Detail: Cloth, Naga. 1500 mm x 970 mm.
Royal Pavilion, Libraries & Museums
WA508450

Fig.4.6.i *above*

An Angami Naga woman weaving a Lohe cloth on a traditional backstrap loom, Zadima village, Kohima district, southern Nagaland, 1992.
Photograph by Vibha Joshi.

Fig.4.6.ii *right*

Stole. Naga, made by Mrs. Pitoli Sema's Weaving and Knitting Society, Dimapur, Kohima district, southern Nagaland, c.1997. Women's stole of new design; acrylic, two-ply yarn, chemical dye. The supplementary weft motif is an improvisation of an old pattern. 1640 mm x 440 mm.
V. Joshi collection

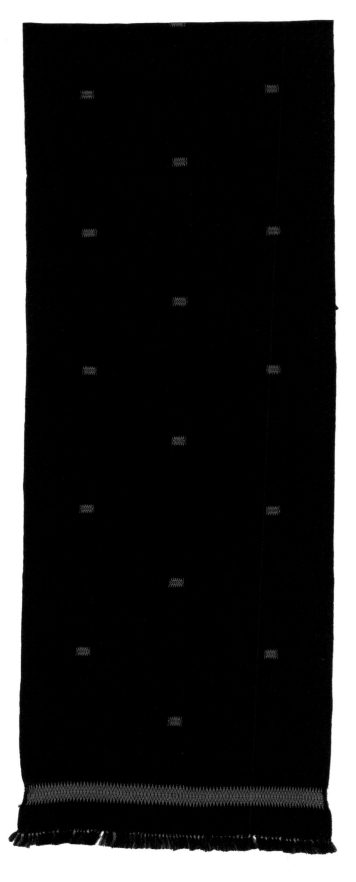

Fig.4.6.iv *above*
Ao Naga men in ceremonial dress during Tsüngremamung festival, Ungma village, Mokokchung district, west Nagaland, 1991. Photograph by Vibha Joshi.

Fig.4.6.iii *right*
Man's apron, probably Sema Naga (Ao, Sangtam and Lotha Nagas also have a similar man's apron). 465 mm x 335 mm. Royal Pavilion, Libraries & Museums WA505179

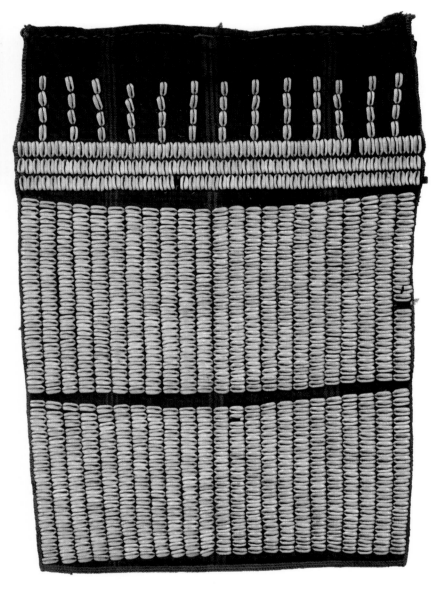

Each Naga ethnic group has a distinct set of fabric, and the cloth denotes variation in age, sex, status and group affiliation. In the past, there were restrictions on motifs that could be woven by a particular ethnic group. As a consequence of accumulated social change resulting from British annexation, the adoption by most Nagas of Christianity, and the Second World War Battle of Kohima; however, these restrictions have loosened. Experimentation in weaving has followed, especially in recent years, with new designs, new colour combinations and use of different yarns, helped by the artistic control provided by the backstrap loom.[3]

Today, weaving is a significant Naga cottage industry. The backstrap loom has remained the most important technique, used for weaving fabric for shawls, sarongs, kilts, sashes, waist belts and shoulder bags.

4.7 Shan State area textiles

Sandra Dudley

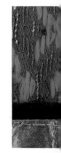

Shan State or formerly, 'the Shan States', covers a very large area bordering China, Laos and Thailand, as well as, within Burma, Mandalay and Sagaing Divisions and Kachin and Karenni (Kayah) States. Historically, the Shan States were divided into principalities, each with its own ruling Sawbwa. The area is home to a number of different groups, many of whose populations straddle the State's borders.[1] Aspects of the textiles and dress of some of these peoples, such as a number of Kachin groups (here including the Lisu), the Akha, the Kayan and the Pa-O, are discussed elsewhere in this chapter. Other groups, such as the Lahu, Riang, Wa, Taungyo and others, cannot be addressed here, but they too continue to be associated with a wonderful array of textiles. In general, Shan State has produced and continues to produce a very wide range of textiles, incorporating a rich variety of decorative techniques. *Ikat*, supplementary weaves and embroidery are all used. Fringing is seen in Riang or Yang Lam ['Black Karen'] women's tunic tops (Fig.4.7.i).[2] Many peoples also employ appliqué in some form, the Lahu, say, utilising a range of coloured felts and printed commercial fabrics to ornament their long, indigo dyed, woman's coat.

Many groups continue to use backstrap looms to produce some or all of the textiles used in the production of dress and bags. The Palaung, for example, a Mon-Khmer group with a clan-based social organisation, use a continuous warp backstrap loom with a very long warp span. Palaung men traditionally wear a Shan-style shirt and wide-legged pants, while women wear a horizontally pinstriped (warp striped) long skirtcloth (the precise colouring and patterning of which is or was said to be clan-dependent),[3] and a short jacket, often together with fabric leg gaiters (Fig.4.7.ii). They also wear headgear, such as a hood and/or a headcloth worn as a turban. For Palaung in the Kalaw area, rather than a hood there is a cap worn by unmarried women, and married women wear the turban.[4] The jackets tend to be made from purchased material, including velvets and satins, and, together with headgear, are decorated with extensive use of sequins, buttons, embroidery, appliqué, piecework, rolled edge-binding and, occasionally, quilting and, for headgear, the attachment of pompoms and other appendages.

Detail: appliqué panels from skirt, Shan, early 20th century. See Fig.4.7.iv.

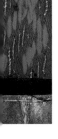

Fig.4.7.i above
'Black Karen woman, head and shoulders,
no pugree.'
Photograph by James Henry Green, 1920s.
Royal Pavilion, Libraries & Museums P0022

Fig.4.7.ii right
Woman's skirt. Palaung, made in Petnehpin
village, near Kalaw. Purchased in 1996. Red
chemically dyed cotton skirt, woven in three
parts on a backstrap loom, with fine yellow,
blue, white and green warp stripes.
1480 mm x 1030 mm.
Royal Pavilion, Libraries & Museums
WA507467

The Tai groups who make up the Shan after whom the state is named, use
automated and non-automated frame looms to produce a variety of textile items.
Men's everyday dress comprises wide cotton trousers and loose fitting shirts,
although in the past high class men sometimes wore Chinese silk brocade robes
(see Maddigan, chapter 6.2). On an everyday basis, most Shan women wore and
by tradition continue to wear a cotton *longyi* with wide and narrow warp stripes.
They also have *longyi* and headcloths more appropriate for special occasions,
incorporating one or more of various decorative techniques such as
supplementary weft designs in silver and gold metallic and other coloured threads,
embroidery, and appliqué. Some women also wear a *longyi* constructed from
three or four portions of fabric rather than the usual two of waistband and
skirtcloth, so that an upper or usually mid panel of textile, embellished with
striping and/or supplementary weft geometric and other designs

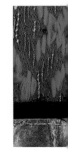

Fig.4.7.iii

Woman's skirt. Shan, made in Thale village, Inle Lake in 1996. Machine woven purple cotton (shot black), with vertically striped polychrome and gold panel incorporating supplementary weft. Purchased as three separate items: plain purple cotton longyi, black cotton waistband, and decorative textile strip; made up into one garment by shop; the mid-section decorative panel is sewn between the two halves of the cut longyi. Northern Shan State style. 1200 mm x 800 mm.

Royal Pavilion, Libraries & Museums WA507455

(often using metallic threads), is stitched above a plain *longyi* piece or between its two halves, cut along the warp (Fig.4.7.ii). This is a style said to be typical of northern Shan State, and especially of the Namkham area, although it is now also made and worn in other parts of Shan State.

Another style of 'traditional' Shan *longyi* comprises a black or other dark, plain cotton ground cloth appliquéd in the lower portion of the skirtcloth with large strips of such materials as gilded leather and plain and printed velvets, silks and cottons. Additional ornamentation on top of and adjacent to these strips can include metal beads and other small metal items (including coins), sequins, and embroidered or coiled silver and gold thread. Sometimes, the overlapping appliquéd strips are smaller, and supplemented with fine gold and polychrome geometric designs in supplementary weft (Fig.4.7.iv, Fig.4.7.v).

Fig.4.7.iv

*Detail of woman's skirt. Shan, made during
the early 20th century. Black cotton skirt,
with two bands of black velvet attached
toward the base. Decorated in a broad,
400 mm appliqué band toward the base of
the cloth. Appliqué consists of polychrome
supplementary weft geometric bands,
patterned silk brocade panels, gilded
goat skin bands, and crimson and green
velvet. Metal sequins and silver beads.
1070 mm x 1425 mm.
Royal Pavilion, Libraries & Museums
G000030b*

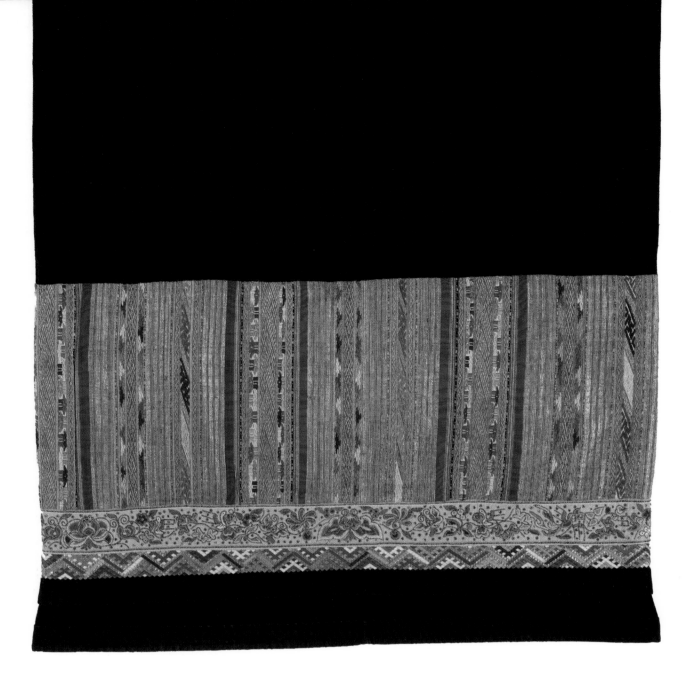
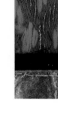

Fig.4.7.v

*Detail of woman's skirt. Shan, collected during
the 1880s. Skirt is black supplementary weft
on black cotton. Lower third of cloth
comprises a broad band of polychrome
supplementary weft pattern, in cotton, silk
and gilt thread, with bands of silk brocade,
decorated with metal sequins. Edged with
fine multicoloured satin ribbons interleaved to
form a raised, basket-weave, appliqué
pattern. 940 mm x 700 mm.*

See chapter 6.2.

Royal Pavilion, Libraries & Museums

WA508311

Fig.4.7.vi

Woman's skirtcloth (longyi). Made by Intha weavers at Inle Lake in 1950. Black silk, with silver weft stripes and white and yellow floral weft ikat patterns, known as zinme.
1600 mm x 1100 mm.
Royal Pavilion, Libraries & Museums WA507514

Around Inle Lake there was and continues to be especially vigorous textile production by Intha and other weavers. In the Inle area, Inpawkhon village particularly is known for its *zinme* ('Chiang Mai', the Thai city) silks. These are worn as *longyi* and incorporate geometric and sometimes naturalistic weft *ikat* designs.[5] The colours of these cloths are usually a warm, complementary blend of reds, greens and yellows (Fig.4.7.vi), and they are made using either plain or twill weave.[6]

Many different sorts of textile shoulder bag have been and continue to be produced in Shan State, ranging from relatively unadorned Palaung bags of undyed cotton, through striped and lettered bags such as those incorporating the woven word 'Inle' in Burmese, to bags with very fine and dense supplementary weft ornamentation over the entire surface of the bag (though not the strap) (Fig.4.7.vii). These Shan bags are a classic style, and the best have supplementary weft decoration of silk. Some are waterproofed inside by the application of a sort of vegetable gum (as are those in the Pitt Rivers Museum, for example).

Fig.4.7.vii

*Bag. Shan, made in the early 20th century.
Silk, with supplementary weft and 'Job's tears'.
Woven in two pieces. A very finely made
example of a classic style of Shan bag.
Sometimes such bags are internally
waterproofed by the application of vegetable
gum. Length, including strap and tassels,
520 mm x 250 mm.
Royal Pavilion, Libraries & Museums
G000192*

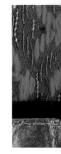

Chapter 5

Burma textiles in local contexts

5.1 Burman court textiles in historical context

Frances Franklin

Descriptions by European emissaries, Burmese court manuscripts, contemporary paintings and royal costumes surviving in national collections, give a vivid picture of the dress codes of Burmese court circles during the Konbaung Dynasty (1752–1885).

A lavish *duyin thindaing* (female state robe) and accessories, dating from the Konbaung period, forms part of the Green collection. Originally collected as the costume of a 'court dancer', the status of this sumptuous ensemble can be more accurately traced using a court *parabaik* (folding manuscript), confirming entitlement for its use by a high-ranking minister's principal wife.[1] The costume is of a style exclusive to the royal family and to those on whom it was bestowed by the king as a special favour (Fig.5.1.i).

King Thibaw Min (r.1878–85) had *parabaik* in his library illustrating and describing in minute detail such costumes and paraphernalia as they were sanctioned for members of the court and for provincial governors and their wives (Fig.5.1.ii). Besides being sumptuously decorated, the form of a robe of state was distinctively non-utilitarian, lacking the ease and comfort of the everyday dress and, with its wing-like projections, bearing a marked similarity to the costumes of *deva* figures in paintings and sculpture, suggesting an intended identification with the heavenly world.[2]

Detail: robe of state of high ranking lady,
Thibaw Min's Court, c.1880. See Fig.5.1.i.

Fig.5.1.ii right

Court parabaik (folding manuscript), showing costume and adornments awarded to the wives of high ranking ministers, court of Thibaw Min, c.1880.
Victoria and Albert Museum
IM 320–1924, pp 47–48

Fig.5.1.i far right

Robe of state and accessories awarded to a high ranking lady of Thibaw Min's Court at Mandalay, c.1880. Detail, showing jacket (duyin thindaing), apron or 'waist string' (kharyan-kyo) and cap (other ornate pieces which form part of this costume, as illustrated in the parabaik Fig.5.1.ii, are not shown here). Imported green silk velvet, lined with yellow satin and decorated with borders of metal braid. Jacket 600 mm x 1308 mm.
Royal Pavilion, Libraries & Museums
WA508344/5, 350

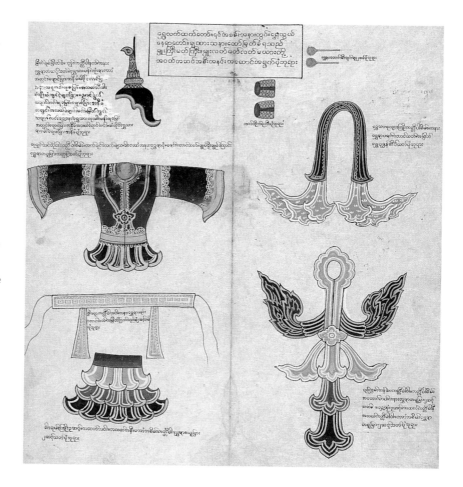

European travellers observed that sumptuary laws were common throughout Southeast Asia. Symes noted that at the Court of Ava in 1800, almost every article, particularly dress, indicated the rank of a person and there were grave penalties for 'him that assumes the insignia of a degree which is not his legitimate right'.[3] While jewelled golden slippers formed part of the regalia of a Burmese monarch, footwear was not part of the court dress awarded to ministers or courtiers as very strict etiquette forbade such items of dress when in audience with the King. Overseeing the royal wardrobe and protocol was an important part of the work of the *achok-wun* (court chamberlain).

At the end of 1854, Mindon Min 'sent a mission of compliment, with presents, to the Governor-General, [of India] Lord Dalhousie'.[4] Sir Arthur Phayre, commissioner of British Burma, acted as interpreter to Ambassador Ashin Nanmadaw Payawun Mingyi. Three watercolours which were presented to the Victoria and Albert Museum by the great niece of Sir Arthur allow us, through the eyes of a Burmese *bagyidaw* (court artist) who accompanied the mission, to witness the pomp with which Burmese ministers travelled.

The *bagyidaw's* observation of detail reveals the manner in which the envoy was attired, as well as much of the world of the Burmese Court during the last years of the Konbaung Dynasty. The ambassador is shown with an entourage carrying his swords, gold umbrellas and receptacles of rank. They are depicted kneeling and in smaller scale than the ambassador, indicating their lesser position.

Fig.5.1.v *above*

Civil Court Dress of Kin Wun Mingyi (Chief Minister), who served Mindon Min and Thibaw Min (1850–1880). Includes a wutlon of crimson imported velvet, lined in apricot silk and decorated with deep borders of floral and foliate patterned yetpya (braid). Length 1120 mm x width (across shoulders) 510 mm. Worn with a pahso embroidered with yellow floss silk on a red cotton ground. 2390 mm x 440 mm. Victoria and Albert Museum IM 43 & 43A–1912

Fig.5.1.iii *top right and right*

The Burmese Minister Nanmadaw Wun's Mission to Calcutta 1854/1855. With Sir Arthur Purves Phayre. Watercolours. Victoria and Albert Museum IS 179 & 181–1950

Two of the watercolours (Fig.5.1.iii) clearly distinguish between the military and civil costumes awarded to ministers and to be worn while attending the King at court or as his representative abroad (Fig.5.1.iv). In the first, the ambassador is splendidly portrayed in his civil court dress consisting of a *wutlon* (robe) over a *pahso* of *acheik luntaya* silk together with a *baung* (hat)(Fig.5.1.v). At his second meeting in Calcutta, the ambassador, seen strolling hand in hand with Phayre, is portrayed in his elaborate and distinctive military court dress, consisting of *myindo myinshei* (jacket and skirt) worn with a *shweipei hkamauk* (helmet) and a *mauk-yu* (skullcap), on this occasion wearing shoes with his *pahso* drawn up to resemble breeches (Fig.5.1.vi).

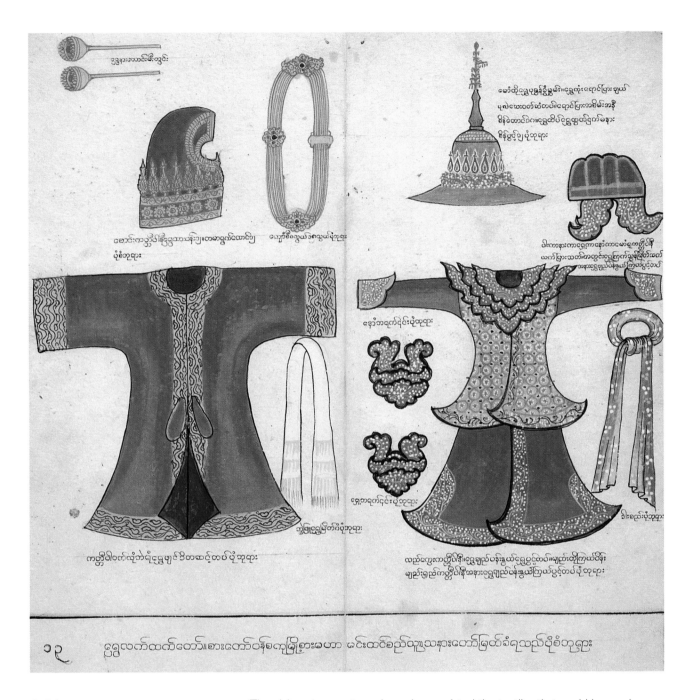

Fig.5.1.iv

Double page of a court parabaik (folding manuscript), showing civil and military court dress and accoutrements awarded to Maha Minhtin Sithu, Governor of Sagu and Lord Chamberlain to Thibaw Min.

Victoria and Albert Museum

IM 320–1924, pp 1–2

The elaborate sumptuary laws also regulated the textiles that could be used generally. The component parts of the most prized of these, the *acheik luntaya*, used for ceremonial or 'dress' *htamein* and *pahso*, were carefully controlled. The best examples of this cloth and, particularly, certain patterns were restricted to the use of the royal family. Green and red were reserved for royal *acheik luntaya*, and pink specifically for royal ladies (Fig.4.2.iii, page 56). *Acheik luntaya* of other colours were permitted for ministers and wealthy Burmese, but weaving for them would be of an inferior quality.[5]

Fig.5.1.vii above

*'Dance of the pin-taing-san' (crown princess),
postcard, Mandalay c.1900. Noel Singer
suggests that the costume was probably a
genuine court costume, which once belonged
to a lady of rank.
Royal Pavilion, Libraries & Museums
WA508418, donated by Noel Singer*

Fig.5.1.vi right

*Military Court Dress of an Atwinwun
(Secretary of State), who served Mindon Min
and Thibaw Min (1850–1885).
Plum and green imported velvet, lined in dark
pink silk, richly decorated with floral and
foliate patterned yetpya and zardozi work.
Length 1280 mm x width (across chest) 450
mm. Worn over a pahso of various coloured
acheik luntaya silk, 4160 mm x 1220 mm.
The minister's position would have been
indicated by the depth and degree of
ornamentation on his cuffs, collar, breast and
back plates.
Victoria and Albert Museum
IM 44 to 44B–1912 & IND.LOST.561*

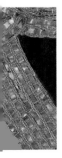

Fig.5.1.viii

Detail from a military costume exhibited at the Burma court of the 1924 Empire Exhibition as '[d]ress worn by Burmese War Minister in the reign of King Thibaw' (Letter, Green Archive, 21 July 1924). Detail shows collar and breast ornamentation, and headpiece, imported maroon silk velvet, lined with floral patterned cotton, and decorated with metal braid.

Royal Pavilion, Libraries & Museums
WA508618

Differences in the style and materials used for various court costumes demonstrated different status. For example, imported textiles and local textiles imitating imports, such as Western velvets and Indian brocades, gold braids and trimmings, were used to distinguish royal from commoner.[6] The gold embroidery stitched to the robes of state by palace artisans is clearly related to Indian *zardozi* work.[7]

While paintings and descriptions attest to high numbers of these spectacular costumes at court, relatively few survive. Before the 1880s, important costumes of deceased parents would probably have been burned in an act of filial piety, and the ashes used in the making of religious texts or images.[8] Most court costumes that have made their way into museum collections did so as a result of conflict. When Mandalay fell in 1885, the court ceased to exist, and there must have been thousands of discarded court robes in the city. There was no local use for these garments, but some were used as photographers' props (Fig.5.1.vii) or collected by discerning or sentimental foreigners.[9] The Victoria and Albert Museum robes from L. M. Parlett were collected by him while he was a Divisional Judge in Burma around 1900. The Green collection court costumes, comprising the *duyin thindaing* described above, and a military court costume (Fig.5.1.viii), were brought to Britain in the early part of the twentieth century and entered the Museum collection in the 1990s. The military court costume was given to a young British army officer in 1885 by the minister he befriended.

5.2 Burmese textile texts: *sazigyo*

Ralph Isaacs

Burmese Buddhists earned merit by commissioning palm leaf manuscripts for monasteries. Each sacred manuscript bundle had its own binding tape.[1]

Introduction and techniques

In the early 1990s, the author found in a stall on the steps of Rangoon's Shwedagon Pagoda several bags full of a tangle of dirty cotton tapes mixed with termite earth. In some derelict monastery, insects and mould must have invaded the *sadaik* manuscript chests, reducing to dust the palm leaf manuscripts but leaving the *sazigyo*, or manuscript binding tapes, more or less intact. Some 50 of these tapes, collected by the author, are now in the Brighton Museum collection. The collection includes undated examples which could be from the early nineteenth century, but those tapes with a woven date are from 1892 to 1928.[2]

In Burma as elsewhere in Southeast Asia, Theravada Buddhist scriptures were inscribed on palm leaves. The folios were strung together between two wooden covers and stored in a cloth bag. Round the whole was wound the *sazigyo*, which was tied by a loop and cord (see Fig.5.2.ii). Between these, the flat tape was often woven with the text of a prayer and a variety of decorative motifs. The tape had two functions: as textile, it bound the manuscript securely in its cloth bag; as text, it recorded the donors' deed of merit.

The flat, double-faced weave between loop and cord can be from 3 to 6 metres long, and 13 to 30 mm wide. It was woven on a tablet loom consisting of a 1.5 metre-long plank, fitted at each end with a movable block of wood. One of these blocks incorporated a peg round which the warp ends are wound, and the other had a roller for winding up the finished part of the tape (Fig.5.2.i).[3] In Mandalay in 1911, weavers of *sazigyo* were observed using 38 tablets of lacquered deerskin.[4] In the Brighton collection, 38 is the most frequent number

Detail: tape. Undated, early 20th century.

Width 35 mm.

Royal Pavilion, Libraries & Museums

Cat 055

of tablets, used in 40 per cent of the tapes. The range is from 28 to 44 tablets, with 80 per cent using between 34 and 42. All the tablets used had four holes.[5] Only two textile structures of the many that are possible are utilised: warp twining and double-faced weave. The latter makes possible the text lettering and the ornamental motifs, including geometric patterns and images of animals and ritual objects (Fig.5.2.iii).

The fineness of the work varies widely, from 38 to 123 warp ends per centimetre width. In the Brighton tapes, the yarn is always cotton,[6] 2- or 3-ply. The coarsest tapes use hand-spun yarn, but all the finer tapes use machine-made thread, probably imported from Britain. The ground colour of the earliest known *sazigyo* was brown, like monks' robes.[7] In 1911 in Mandalay, weavers used yellow for the text, on a black ground.[8] Plain red and indigo blue are common. In all these 'two-colour' tapes, the text is in undyed natural cotton. After about 1890 many colours of imported yarn began to be used, and some tapes dated 1907 use six or more colours (Fig.5.2.iv).

Texts and motifs

Sazigyo are generally in Burmese,[9] but the initial invocation at least is in Pali, the language of the Theravada Buddhist scriptures. Most texts open with a standard invocation of auspiciousness for the donation (Fig.5.2.vi). The main text that follows can be up to 5 metres long, with 80 or more four-syllable *pada* verses. In many long texts, the cumulative total of verses is given after every ten verses, and each set of figures (10, 20, 30, etc.) is accompanied by a neat woven image of a parrot or a fish (Fig.5.2.vii). Verses praise the donor couple and name their close family. Finally, in a set phrase the donors declare that they seek *Nibbana* (*Nirvana*), and call on human and celestial beings to applaud their deed and to share its merit. At the end of the text the date of the donation may appear, and also the total verse-count (Fig.5.2.viii). The weaver may add her name and even the price she asked (Fig.5.2.ix). A few tapes also show the Pali title of the manuscript for which they were made. In the finest tapes, the lettering is wonderfully neat and small: the round parts can be 3 mm in diameter (Fig.5.2.iv).

A specimen text is given below in English translation:[10]

Brighton collection cat 050 (2-colour, text natural on carmine; length 3650 mm, width 22mm).[11] Singer uses evidence in the text to date this tape to between 1874 and 1878, when the donor, U Kaung, the Kin Wun Mingyi, was close to King Mindon and at the height of his power.[12] He had visited Europe in 1872, survived with reduced influence under King Thibaw (1878–85), and was respected and consulted by the British after the deposition of the Burmese monarchy in 1885. He died in 1908. Mi Mi Gyi, 1993 p. 36, text no. 4, is a very similar text from a tape donated by U Kaung, the Kin Wun Mingyi.

Fig.5.2.i

The manuscript tapes were woven on a tablet loom consisting of a 1.5 metre-long plank, fitted at each end with a moveable block of wood to hold the warp threads. Complex text designs were formed using between 24 and 44 leather tablets, each having four holes.

Photographed by Scherman in 1911 and published in 1913.

St. Gallen Museum, Switzerland

Let this be proclaimed and made known. As the Buddha, Lord of the Universe, predicted, this land of Mandalay has become the sacred centre for the teaching of the *sasana*. This holy land of Mandalay has been granted to the King in accordance with his acquired virtues and power, and he has in addition conquered hundreds of realms throughout the world. The King's great Counsellor and Minister, the *Min thadoe mingyi maha Minhla sithu kyaw* (one of his many royal titles), the Kin Wun Mingyi, tax-collector of paddy-fields and other agricultural produce, Army Minister and Commander of Artillery, who is comparable to a brilliant ruby in the high mountain, together with his graceful wife, commissioned the writing of the scriptures of the great Lord Buddha, and prays to attain *Nibbana* without obstacles. May all human and celestial beings have their share in the merit of this deed.

In Burmese art, little ornament is entirely devoid of religious meaning. Even simple woven block-patterns most often have nine elements – the ancient *navaratna* or 'nine gems' motif. Block-motifs occur in groups, and a single tape can have dozens (Fig.5.2.iii). Often the blocks separate the more elaborate pictorial motifs. A few very elaborate tapes have up to 50 of these. Pictorial images of stags, horses, elephants, frogs, fish and tortoises have no obvious religious significance.[13] Most images, however, depict ritual objects associated with merit-earning acts. The woven text is itself a meritorious deed, preceded and followed by sequences of images which imitate the stages of the ritual. Thus at the start of the tape, after some introductory block motifs, the first image is usually a pair of guardian *nats* or of *chintheis,* the mythical bearded lions which flank the stairway up to the pagoda platform. A sacred fig tree *nyaungbin* appears on the tape, as on the platform, where watering it is a pious act (Fig.5.2.iii). All of these images, and others,

Fig.5.2.ii

Binding tape wound round its manuscript, with the loop and cord shown here untied, dated 1906. Width 22 mm.

Royal Pavilion, Libraries & Museums

Cat 028

are topped by a *hti* umbrella or by a *pyathat* multi-tiered roof, both attributes of the Buddha and royalty. After the text announcing the donation, the tape then depicts a round bell with its deer antler striker and a *kyizi* gong and hammer, mirroring the conclusion of active religious duty in which the donor strikes a bell thrice, to call on spirits and nearby humans to share in the merit of the deed.[14] Next comes a *Nat* figure holding a staff to strike the ground, to placate the subterranean spirits and offer them too a share in the merit. The last image to appear on the tape is the *tagundaing*, the tall flagpole with *hintha* bird atop, visible from a distance as the pilgrim approaches or leaves the pagoda (Fig.5.2.v, Fig.5.2.x).[15]

Weavers based their charges on the length of text woven, or on the number of verses, and the price asked for the work sometimes appears on the tape just after the total number of verses. A very skilful weaver may add her name (Fig.5.2.ix).

Manuscript binding tapes, *sazigyo*, are truly textile texts. Many illuminate the social and religious context in which the donors conceived their acts of merit. The finest of these tapes are technically and aesthetically superb, a monument to the skill and flair of Burmese weavers.

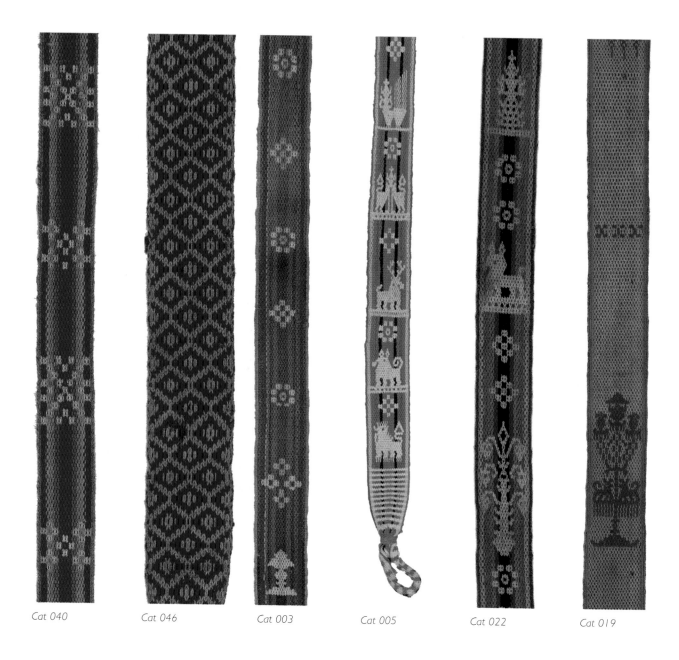

Cat 040   Cat 046   Cat 003   Cat 005   Cat 022   Cat 019

Fig.5.2.iii *left to right*
Details of tapes showing block ornaments
and vertical pictorial images:
Cat 040, undated, c.1920s, no text, only
geometrical block ornament.
Width 15 mm.
Cat 046, undated, early 20th century,
diamond patterns at the end of text.
Width 23 mm.
Cat 003, dated 1906, block ornaments, most
of nine elements. Width 14 mm.

Cat 005, dated 1907, from top: kinnara,
manuthiha, stag, horse and lion; probably no
religious significance. Width 12 mm.
Cat 022, dated 1907, sacred fig tree in pot,
symbol of Buddha. Width 15 mm.
Cat 019, undated c.1870, (reverse) elaborate
stand with lions, religious significance
unknown. Width 16 mm.
Royal Pavilion, Libraries & Museums

Cat 043

Cat 044

Cat 017

Cat 014

Fig.5.2.iv *top to bottom*
Details of tapes showing woven text:
Cat 043, 19th century, text natural on indigo.
Width 21 mm.
Cat 044, undated, early 20th century,
multicoloured, text natural on blue.
Width 14 mm.
Cat 017, dated 1907, text natural on red,
square lettering. Width 11 mm.
Cat 014, dated 1907, 6-colour elaborate
text. Width 14 mm.
Royal Pavilion, Libraries & Museums

Fig.5.2.v *left to right*
Details of tapes showing large
vertical images:
Cat 003, dated 1906. The last image on this
tape is an elaborate flag pole with hintha
bird and streamer tagundaing. Width 13 mm.
Cat 014, dated 1907. Width 14 mm.
Cat 041, undated. Width 16 mm.
Cat 027, dated 1912, 10 verses.
Width 13 mm.
Royal Pavilion, Libraries & Museums

Cat 003   *Cat 014*   *Cat 041*   *Cat 027*

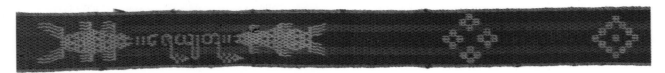

Cat 039

Cat 041

Cat 014

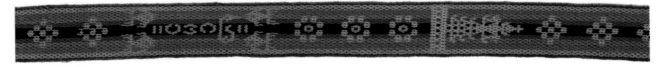

Cat 022

Fig.5.2.vi *top pair*
Details of tapes showing initial invocation,
'Zeyattu':
Cat 039, late 19th century. Zeyattu flanked
by fish. Width 16 mm.
Cat 041, late 19th century. Zeyattu in fancy
cartouche. Width 16 mm.
Royal Pavilion, Libraries & Museums

Fig.5.2.vii *bottom pair*
Details of tapes showing verse counts;
cumulative totals may be given in the text at
every ten verses:
Cat 014, dated 1907. Verse count with
parrot every 10 verses. Width 14 mm.
Cat 022, dated 1907. Final total '86 verses'
between two pairs of fish. Width 15 mm.
Royal Pavilion, Libraries & Museums

Cat 017

Cat 022

Cat 028

Cat 028

Fig.5.2.viii *top pair*
Details of tapes showing dates of donation,
and so of weaving:
Cat 017, dated 1907, in Burmese and
English lettering between pointing hands.
Width 11 mm.
Cat 022, dated 1269 Burmese era (1907).
Width 15 mm.
Royal Pavilion, Libraries & Museums

Fig.5.2.ix *below*
Cat 028, dated 1906. Details of tape
showing weaver's signature; 'May Yu's
handwork' and '67 verses: price 2 rupees,
8 annas'. Width 22 mm.
Royal Pavilion, Libraries & Museums

Fig.5.2.x left to right

Details of tapes depicting ritual objects associated with merit-earning acts:

Cat 022, dated 1907, showing round bell with antler striker. Width 15 mm.

Cat 005, dated 1907, showing round bell with 2 nat supporters, flat kyizi bell with 3 birds atop. Width 12 mm.

Cat 017, dated 1907, showing nat figure with staff, 3 hti umbrellas atop. Width 11 mm.

Royal Pavilion, Libraries & Museums

Cat 022   Cat 005   Cat 017

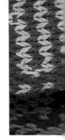

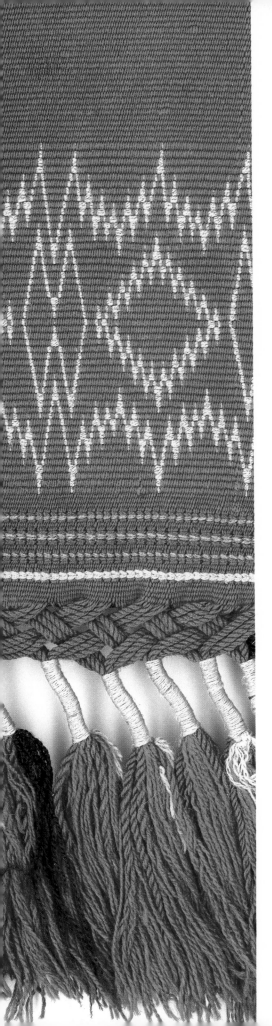

5.3 Design, meaning and identity in Naga textiles: continuity and change

Vibha Joshi

Green visited Nagas in the Tamanthi and Kanti areas only once, and in his dissertation admits 'I have very little firsthand knowledge of the Nagas'.[1] He focuses on Nagas' relative nakedness rather than on their textiles (e.g. Fig.5.3.i). Nonetheless, the overall Brighton collection does include Naga textiles, mostly Sema Naga (Fig.5.3.ii, Fig.5.3.iii). Furthermore, hand woven textiles have been important in strengthening and negotiating what it means to be 'Naga'. Nagas are traditionally cultivators and, formerly, warriors and headhunters. In different Naga ethnic groups, these two activities have influenced the development of vibrant textiles and their symbolism.[2] The adoption of Christianity and more recent social and political changes has also influenced textile design and meaning, and the relationship between textiles and identity. This case study examines some of these influences on 'traditional' Naga cloth.

Traditionally, Naga textiles denote both group affiliation and individual status. Motifs on the cloth are generally group-specific, although Naga groups that live in close proximity and share myths of migration and/or origin, have similar cloths. Furthermore, certain kinds of cloth (as well as ceremonial ornaments) were, in the past, traded among different Naga communities; e.g. a red body cloth with black stripes (Fig.5.3.iv) and a median white band with painted motifs, is used by the Ao, Rengma and Lotha Nagas. Similarly, a blue cloth with deeper blue stripes is common to the Ao, Yimchungrü, Sangtam and Khiamungan Nagas. Cloth may also communicate age group, social status in terms of bravery (e.g. warrior's shawl, Fig.5.3.v), prosperity and shows of hospitality within the community (e.g. rich men and women's shawls, where the right to wear is acquired after having given a series of feasts to clansfolk from one's own and neighbouring villages). Textiles also often relate to the wearer's gender: patterns for some men's and women's cloths are similar among the Angami, but differ considerably in other Naga groups.

Detail: Lohe cloth, Angami Naga. See Fig.5.3.ix.

Fig.5.3.i

'Group of Nagas' photographed by James Henry Green, 1920s. Green wrote in his dissertation in 1934 that he had very little firsthand knowledge of the Nagas, and chose to draw attention to racial comparisons with Nmai valley peoples, rather than to make observations about dress and textiles.
Royal Pavilion, Libraries & Museums 0585

Christianity and colonialism

Amongst Burmese Nagas, Christianity was introduced primarily by Naga evangelists from the Indian side of the border. Indian Naga nationalists, or 'undergrounds', have continued to promote Christianity on the Burmese side.[3] The first conversions to Christianity in the nineteenth century and onwards were accompanied by severe religious sanctions against activities that could be associated with traditional religious beliefs. These sanctions had a direct effect on clothing, as some cloths could be worn only by those who had acquired status by showing prowess in war or head-hunting, or by giving feasts of merit, all associated with the 'heathen' way of life that required performance of non-Christian rituals. On the Indian side, for example, the American Baptist Mission opened schools, and applied to all students sanctions against wearing traditional clothing.

J. H. Hutton and J. P. Mills, British Political Officers in the Naga Hills on the Indian side between 1915 and 1937, were against this trend and passed an order that only if students continued to wear traditional dress would the missionaries be allowed to run schools. Where Hutton and Mills had direct control, they exercised their power to retain as much of the 'traditional' outfit as was possible. Government interpreters, for example, were forbidden to wear western-style clothes. Nonetheless, women had already begun to wear blouses over their sarongs, and men were adopting shirts and shorts. Ironically, it was the British administration that introduced the mill-made red woollen blankets that ended up symbolising the office of the GB or *gaonbura*, i.e. the government appointed chief of the village. Similarly, red waistcoats came to identify the office of the government interpreters or *dubhashi* at the District Commissioner's court. On the Indian side of the border, the offices of GB and *dubhashi* have continued to the present time, as has the wearing of the red shawls (Fig.5.3.vi).

Fig.5.3.ii

Baldric or sash. Sema Naga. Indigo blue cloth,
decorated with yellow orchid stems and red
and yellow fringe of naturally dyed goats' hair.
It is worn (in the past by warriors) during
ceremonial dances. 365 mm x 735 mm.
Royal Pavilion, Libraries & Museums
WA505182

Like Mills and Hutton, Fürer-Haimendorf, the Austrian anthropologist who worked among the Konyak Nagas in the 1930s and 1970s, found it incongruous to see Nagas wearing Western clothing. After a visit to an Ao Naga village, he wrote:

> People with serious faces came out of the chapel. There was the "pastor", a skinny young man in khaki shorts, and a mauve coat. Some of his flock had also adopted shorts, but the rest of the community was content to emphasize their allegiance to the new doctrine by wearing plain dark-blue cloths, while the women wore white blouses, imported from the plains, with their Naga skirts. The Ao's most cherished and valued possessions, the pride of generations, lay unheeded and scattered in the jungle – ivory armlets, necklaces of boar's tusks, cowrie shells, head dresses and artistically woven coloured cloths, all discarded because they belong to the old times.[4]

Things became more complicated, however, than Christian converts simply preferring to wear Western clothing. In certain Naga groups, converts began to wear cloths that could traditionally be worn only by those men who had taken a head or given a series of feasts of merit. In his official tour diary of June 1934, Hutton describes the conflict between Christian and non-Christian Sema Naga villagers over the wearing of ceremonial cloth, and his suggestion for settling it:

> The question of the patterns of cloths is giving trouble. Certain patterns are worn by householders who have performed certain social ceremonies and by their

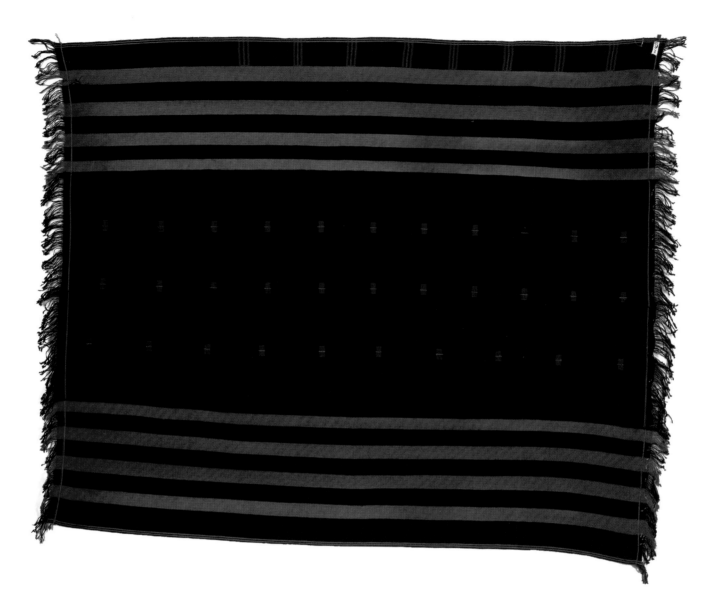

Fig.5.3.iii

Man's cloth. Sema Naga.

1600 mm x 1310 mm.

Royal Pavilion, Libraries & Museums

WA505174

unmarried sons; when the boy marries he ceases to wear the cloth until he has qualified for it. The pattern is very popular and Christians have started wearing it without qualification which has scandalized the Ancients. Both sides came to me about it. I ruled that Ancients had the right to it, but that provided some recognisable alteration was made in the pattern no exception would be taken to Christians wearing similar ones. I suggested a red cross in the middle of the black ground which was accepted without demur by those present.[5]

Naga dress today

Today, although Western dress is part of everyday clothing, traditional style cloth is worn in addition, commonly in the form of a wrap (Fig.5.3.vii). Past restrictions on who could wear these cloths no longer hold sway, and people from different

Fig.5.3.v right

*Yimchungrü Naga men in ceremonial dress
wearing the warrior's cloth, during the annual
festival of Metemneo, Kuthur village, Tuensang
district, east Nagaland, 1991.
Photograph by Vibha Joshi.*

Fig.5.3.iv below right

*Ao Naga men in ceremonial dress at
Tsüngremamung festival, Ungma village,
Mokokchung district, northwest Nagaland,
1991. Man on far left is wearing the
warriors' cloth (Tsungkotep).
Photograph by Vibha Joshi.*

communities use motifs from each other's cloth. Furthermore, colours and designs
used for cloths are continually changing. Such innovation, however, is not new:
'traditional' cloths evolved in the past as well as now, and as a result what is meant
by 'traditional' is open to question. A recent Sema Naga rich woman's cloth
(*Hekhutha Khum*), for example, was stated by its maker to be 'traditional'.
However, the entry for a very similar cloth collected by Mills in 1932 and now
in the Pitt Rivers Museum, reads:

> Woman's cloth with pale blue bands between narrow strips of red, orange-yellow
> + black with double cross bands of red + yellow worked on one side of the
> cloth forming a check pattern. A recently invented pattern growing in popularity.[6]

Fig.5.3.vi *right*

The elderly man in the centre is wearing the red shawl that depicts his official status of Gaonbura. Chakhasang Naga, Losapehu village, Phek district, southeast Nagaland, 1990.
Photograph by Vibha Joshi.

Fig.5.3.vii *below right*

A Khiamungan Naga elder with his grandson. Note the contrast in dress and the western clothes hanging on the clothesline: the elderly man is wearing a traditional loincloth and sports the chest and arm tattoos of a headhunter. Noklak village, Tuensang district, eastern Nagaland (near Indo-Burma border), 1991.
Photograph by Vibha Joshi.

Fig.5.3.viii *far right above*

Lohe cloth, Angami Naga. Older combination worn by Mao Nagas of northeast Manipur, India. 1680 mm x 1150 mm.
Royal Pavilion, Libraries & Museums WA505185

Fig.5.3.ix *far right below*

Lohe cloth, Angami Naga. Silk and cotton, with red and green warp stripes.
A detail of this cloth at the beginning of this chapter shows the supplementary weft motif, which is woven only at one end along the breadth of the cloth, the other end being left plain. 1830 mm x 1030 mm.
Royal Pavilion, Libraries & Museums WA508335

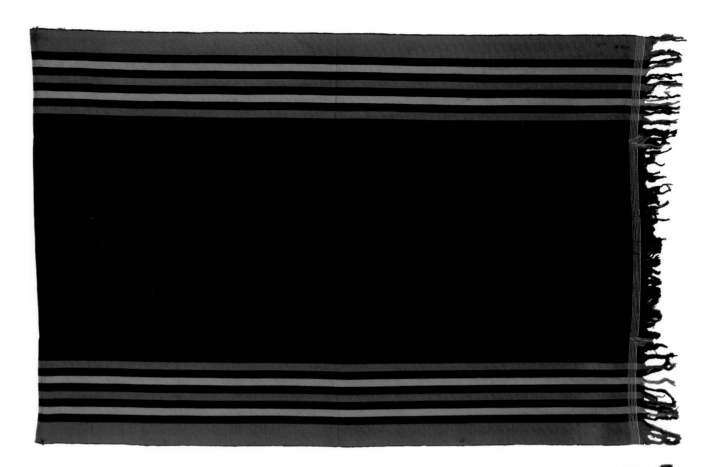

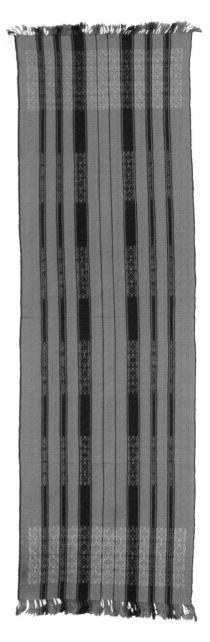

Fig.5.3.xi above

Woman's stole (konken pemo: literally 'orange cloth'). Lotha Naga, produced by Mrs. Thunebeni Ngullie's weaving co-operative, Terhuneke Women Weaving and Knitting Co-operative Society, Kohima town, Kohima district, southern Nagaland, c.1997. Acrylic, two-ply yarn, chemical dye, with an improvised supplementary weft motif based on the traditional geometric motif (lumthen). 1720 mm x 490 mm.

V. Joshi collection

In general, comparing old and new textiles often shows that what is considered 'traditional' now was an innovation 60 or 70 years ago, in terms of colour, design elements, or both. Indeed, in new cloths earlier design elements may simply be repeated more frequently or modified in some way, such as by being elongated. The colour combination of the Angami *Lohe* cloth changed from yellow and orange on a black background to pink and green and red and green on black (Fig.5.3.viii to Fig.5.3.x). Certain colour combinations, although used in cloths that continue to incorporate traditional motifs, come into vogue for some years and are then replaced by another. The Lotha's woman's cloth, for example, was in 1990–91 fashionable in bottle green and red, while in 1997, orange and light green were in vogue (Fig.5.3.xi). Between these periods, cobalt blue and red with white motifs had become popular.

But not only colour and design change over time. Some traditional cloths have gained new meanings[7]. The Chakhasang warrior's cloth, for example, is now known as the educated cloth, to be worn only by graduate men. Similarly, by 1997 the Angami Nagas had designed a sarong, with black body, yellow-orange border and green motif, for graduate women. This is a modification of the traditional cloth that had an orange border and black body, and was presented to a woman of great achievement by her clansfolk.

Textiles are now part of every official gift exchange, just as they were part of traditional gift exchanges. Nowadays this includes Christian exchanges, so that when a delegation from the Northeast church on the Indian side went to meet the Pope, they presented him with Naga cloths and other accessories that traditionally were part of the headhunter's dress. Christian ceremonies too often now involve 'traditional' cloth: for example, the Angami white *Lohramoshü* cloth that traditionally has eight float weft motifs of different designs (these days a single design is repeated), was used as the ordination robe for the first Angami priest, ordained in 1989 (Fig.5.3.xii).

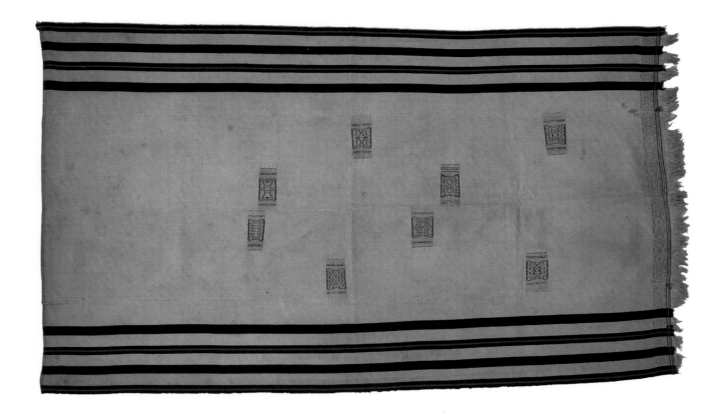

Fig.5.3.xii above

Ceremonial cloth (lohra moshü), Angami Naga. The cloth depicts peace and the motif represents stylised human figures and spears. 1720 mm x 1000 mm.

Royal Pavilion, Libraries & Museums WA508334

Fig.5.3.x above left

Angami Naga women returning from Sunday church service, wearing Lohe sarong and wrap with stripes of different shades of pink (two-ply, mixed wool, cashmilon, chemical dye). Kohima town, Kohima district, southern Nagaland, 1993.

Photograph by Vibha Joshi.

Cloth plays an active role in the strengthening and revival of ethnic identity among Nagas on both sides of the India/Burma border. Nonetheless, outside museum collections very few old cloths are seen today. Unlike some other Southeast Asian communities, Nagas do not preserve textiles as heirlooms. The traditional system of burial required display – and eventual disintegration – of the deceased's personal belongings on the grave. Consequently, now as in the past many traditional designs are not available to young Naga weavers for reference. Nonetheless, textile design continues to evolve, and cloth continues to reflect social relations, identities and values.

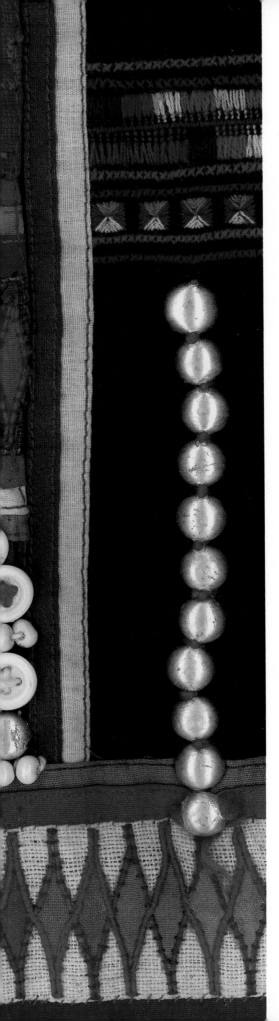

5.4 Clothing and courtship: Akha textiles in social context

Mika Toyota

According to the Akha oral historical record, the Akha originally came from southwest China, where the majority of the population still lives. In all, some 1,260,000 Akha as a part of Hani, the third largest officially recognised minority in Yunnan province, are still located there (Chinese official statistics in 1996). From there, many have migrated southwards over the last two hundred years or so, due to political turmoil in the Yunnan region in the mid-nineteenth century and the crossfire between communists and the Kuomintang (KMT) forces in the 1950s. The total population of people calling themselves 'Akha', and/or officially categorised as 'Aini/Hani', in southwest China, north Burma, north Thailand, north Laos and north Vietnam, is now estimated at around 2,350,000.[1]

Akha textiles have always been used, literally, as the thread of social relations and networks. The ways in which Akha textiles fit into traditional courtship practice, for example, illustrate this well. Green took two posed photographs of Akha couples courting (Fig.5.4.i), and here, I discuss traditional Akha courtship practice as described to me by my informants in Thailand, Burma and China during my field research, from 1994–98.[2] While radical social changes have taken place in the last 50 years or so,[3] this form of courtship was practised among the Akha in Thailand up to the beginning of the 1970s. Hence, what follows is written in the past tense, but according to informants, this courtship practice is still adhered to today by Akha residing in the deep mountain areas in Burma and Laos.

Young Akha men were expected to marry girls from villages other than their own, so when men reached adolescence they travelled in groups to visit other villages during the dry season, in the period between the Akha New Year and rice planting. This was not only an important rite of passage for the boys and an opportunity for them to find a prospective wife, it also helped widen their knowledge of the area and teach them the courtesies involved in meeting strangers. They also needed to look attractive to impress the girls. According to my informant,[4] before entering the village the young men would bathe in the river and put on fresh costumes that they carried with them in shoulder bags. Although Akha men are far more subdued in their dress than women, they would wear

Detail: Woman's jacket. Lomi Akha, Kengtung.
See Fig.5.4.iv.

Fig.5.4.i

'Kaws [Akha] dancing with pipe.'
Green took posed photographs showing Akha
couples courting, traditional courtship
practices which have survived to a small
extent in Akha communities in the deep
mountain areas in Burma.
Photograph by James Henry Green, 1920s.
Royal Pavilion, Libraries & Museums 1584

their best sets of baggy trousers and long-sleeved jackets on these occasions. It
normally takes a few years to make such a dress set, and to wear a freshly made
full dress is a special and important act. An elderly informant could still recall
proudly wearing a new jacket that had been lovingly made by his mother for this
special occasion in which he became a 'man'. He remembered it as the first time
he wore a brand new outfit. 'The touch of the cloth was still nicely firm and it had
the fresh indigo smell with it.' What he found embarrassing was that the freshly
dyed indigo blue stained parts of the body that were sweating. This Akha man
thus had a deep memory of his rite of passage, and the memory itself was
strongly tied to the physicality of his costume and the textile from which it was
made (Fig.5.4.ii).

Additionally, the young men would wear elaborate silver ornaments, such as rings,
bracelets, chains and neckrings (Fig.5.4.iii). Although Akha society is often projected
as 'egalitarian', there has always been relative opulence alongside poverty. This
social differentiation, based on status and wealth, was expressed in costume. The
amount of silver ornaments on outfits, for example, was not simply decoration but
also an indication of wealth. According to my informants, it was common for the
poor boys to borrow these silver ornaments to dress up for the courtship
occasion in order to impress girls and their parents. When seeking a bride, the
boy was also advised to observe the amount of silver on the girl's outfit to
establish whether she would be a suitable match for his own family in terms of
wealth. Furthermore, wealth was also indicated by carrying a red textile used as a
blanket (*habune* in Akha), that in the past only the rich could afford.

During these village visits and after dinner in the evening, villagers and visitors
would congregate at *Deh Hawng*, a village meeting ground where dancing, singing
love songs and courtship took place (Fig.5.4.i). Bamboo benches were usually
placed around the sides of the community ground and everyone in the village,

young and old, male and female, sat there or gathered around the fire. While being gazed at by their male visitors, the young women danced in a circle facing inward, showing the colourful backs of their outfits which were highlighted by the fire against the dark of the night (see illustration at head of chapter). Wearing a sash (Fig.5.4.v) and a full headdress implied that the girl was mature enough to marry, while a cap intimated her unreadiness, thus clearly identifying her social stage of life in her costume (Fig.5.4.vi). The altered status of the bride at the wedding ceremony was in turn displayed by changing her skirt into wearing undyed white instead of blue-black (Fig.5.4.vii). After the ceremony, she normally wears the blue-black skirt. However, she retains the white skirt until the time of her menopause in her 50s, after which she may be entitled to play a new role in the annual rice rituals, wearing her white skirt.

Fig.5.4.iii right

'Kaw [Akha] man and girl holding hands.'
Photograph by James Henry Green, 1920s.
Royal Pavilion, Libraries & Museums 1517

Fig.5.4.iv below

Woman's jacket. Lomi Akha, made in Sungsak
village, near Kengtung, Shan State in 1996.
Indigo dyed cotton jacket made of four
pieces, appliquéd and embroidered in
polychrome using repeating contrasting
diamonds and triangle motifs.
Decorated with seeds, 'Job's tears' and
buttons. 680 mm x 460 mm.
Royal Pavilion, Libraries & Museums
WA507483

Akha women used to wear a full-set costume, including headdress, not only on special occasions but also when they were working in the fields and even whilst sleeping. Costume also had significant influence on the male's choice of partner. The needlework on a girl's costume was regarded by Akha men as good guide to the character, taste and quality of a woman. The skill of the needlework was important in establishing whether or not she was neat, hardworking and careful. Akha women were supposed to master the whole process of dress production around the age of sixteen to eighteen years, and they expressed their skills and maturity by wearing the full dress made by themselves.

Pre-marital sex within young, recognised couples was not prohibited. However, having a child outside of marriage was taboo. Giving birth to an illegitimate child was considered a disgrace not only for the girl's family, but also for the whole village, and had to be prevented. To avoid this occurrence, adolescent girls were advised by female elders to obtain some of their boyfriend's possessions, such as textiles, whose specifics could be traced to a particular family, to be used

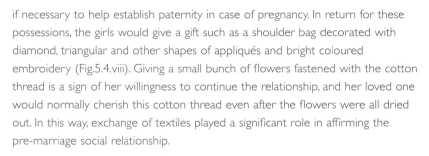

if necessary to help establish paternity in case of pregnancy. In return for these possessions, the girls would give a gift such as a shoulder bag decorated with diamond, triangular and other shapes of appliqués and bright coloured embroidery (Fig.5.4.viii). Giving a small bunch of flowers fastened with the cotton thread is a sign of her willingness to continue the relationship, and her loved one would normally cherish this cotton thread even after the flowers were all dried out. In this way, exchange of textiles played a significant role in affirming the pre-marriage social relationship.

In the past, it was men who travelled to find their brides and to engage in trade. However, with the growing value of Akha handicrafts and textiles in the tourist market, women are increasingly involved in textile and handicraft trade, even across the borders. Since women have always monopolised the whole manufacturing sequence of textiles, when Chiang Mai developed to become the tourist centre of northern Thailand in the 1970s and '80s, they came to play the key role in the 'hill tribes' handicraft industry, not just as producers but also as distributors. Though in most cases the Akha women's skills and labour are exploited by middlemen in the tourist industry, some Akha women have managed to establish their own shops, shrewdly negotiating prices in their own language, and making use of their own transnational social networks across China, Burma and Thailand to promote their wares. It should be said, however, that not all transactions are commercial: Akha women are generally reluctant to sell textiles which have important social significance or to which they have a personal attachment. One of my own Akha acquaintances, for example, refused to take money for a garment, saying, 'I would rather give it to you as a gift (than sell it) because this value can not be measured by money'. However, in the face of the current situation of desperate impoverishment and political insecurity, many Akha have little choice but to sell even their most cherished textiles in the tourist market in order to survive.

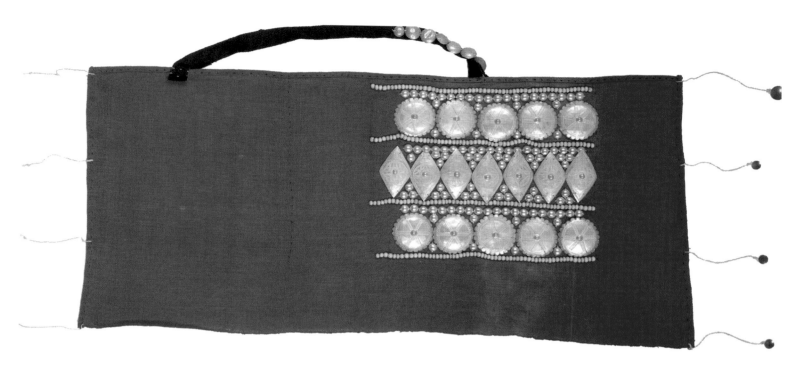

Fig.5.4.vi above

'Mixed group of Kaws [Akha].'
The costume of Akha women clearly
identified their social stage of life; for
example, the full headdress indicated that
the girl was mature enough to marry, while a
cap intimated her unreadiness.
Photograph by James Henry Green, 1920s.
Royal Pavilion, Libraries & Museums 1547

Fig.5.4.v above left
Bodice. Lomi Akha, made in Sungsak village,
near Kengtung, Shan State in 1996.
Red cotton, decorated at front with silver
plaques and disks beaten from Burmese pya
coins. Also includes seed decoration. Single
indigo cotton strap, decorated with silver disks
and a silver-coloured plastic coin from China.
760 mm x 350 mm.
Royal Pavilion, Libraries & Museums
WA507484

Fig.5.4.vii below left
New skirt, pleats still held in place with
cotton threads. Lomi Akha, made in Sungsak
village, near Kengtung, Shan State in 1996.
This full, pleated, new, indigo dyed cotton skirt
would be worn with an elasticated waist,
once the pleat holders have been removed.
500 mm x 430 mm.
Royal Pavilion, Libraries & Museums
WA507485

Fig.5.4.viii right
Bag. Akha, made in Kentung, Shan State in
1996. Black cotton decorated with
polychrome appliqué, crossstitch, pompoms
and seeds. 700 mm (including strap), x
300 mm.
Royal Pavilion, Libraries & Museums
WA507494

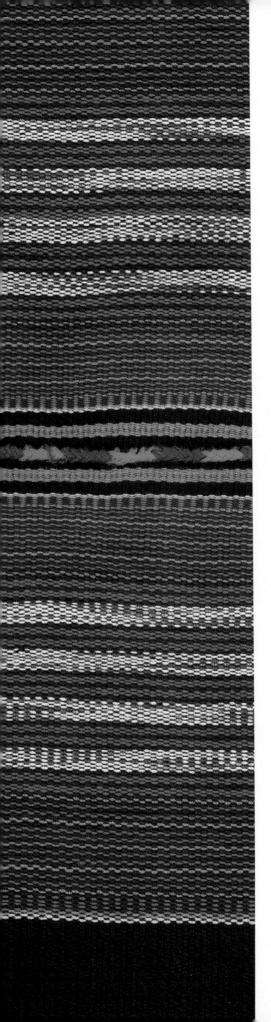

5.5 Textiles in exile:
Karenni refugees in Thailand

Sandra Dudley

Introduction

It is generally accepted that textiles, dress and textile production have significant cultural importance and meaning. This is no less true in exile, where textiles and their manufacture can play an important part in defining people's ideas of who they are and of the home they have left behind. This case study, based on the author's field research, examines textiles in exile and ideas of 'home' in the context of Karenni refugee camps on the Burmese border in northwest Thailand.[1,2]

Karenni people have been fleeing Karenni (Kayah) State and seeking refuge in Thailand in significant numbers since 1989. In early 1996, the total Karenni refugee population was about 5,500. By the end of 1997, it had doubled to 11,000,[3] a dramatic increase that resulted from the arrival of new refugees in one particular Karenni camp (Camp 2) after May 1996 because of forced 'village relocations' inside Karenni State. Conditions in this camp deteriorated rapidly, and great demands were placed upon space and all people concerned, with new refugees experiencing high morbidity and mortality rates.

Displacement of 'the Karenni' into Thailand has thrown together people who differ markedly. Most of the numerous self-defined ethnic groups and associated languages present in the camps originate in Karenni State and refer to themselves as 'Karenni', but simultaneously describe themselves as ethnically distinct; i.e. there is no problem in holding more than one identity at once, and 'Karenni' is used as an umbrella term. The Karenni groups are ethnically and linguistically part of the wider Karenic family, yet they are politically and historically distinct from the more numerous Karen from Karen State (Kawthoolei). Most Karenni groups originate in Karenni State but otherwise exhibit great diversity in ethnicity and language, socio-economic and educational backgrounds, religion, political awareness, and

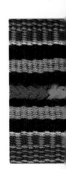

Detail: woman's skirtcloth (ninaw or niperthouk). Paku Karen, made in Karenni Refugee Camp 5, Thailand. See Fig.5.5.i.

Fig.5.5.i *right*

Woman's skirtcloth (ninaw or niperthouk).
Paku Karen, made in Karenni Refugee Camp
5, Thailand, by Oo Mey, and purchased in the
camp from Naw Sarah (name changed),
1997. Cotton and polycotton, woven on a
continuous warp backstrap loom, with warp
ikat patterning within central white stripes.
Traditionally worn with a blouse like that in
Fig.5.5.ii. 1720 mm x 1045 mm.
Royal Pavilion, Libraries & Museums
WA508061, collected by Sandra Dudley

Fig.5.5.ii *left*

Woman's blouse (hsei lat). Paku Karen, from
Ray-loh village, Karen State. Bought in
Karenni Refugee Camp 5, Thailand, from
Naw Sarah, 1997. Embroidery on
commercially produced cloth, with zigzag
trim. Traditionally such shirts were worn only
by married women, but they are now also
worn by single women. Traditionally worn with
a skirtcloth like that in Fig.5.5.i.
510 mm x 580 mm.
Royal Pavilion, Libraries & Museums
WA508067, collected by Sandra Dudley

the experience of displacement itself. Displacement has thus thrown together diverse groups who previously had fewer contacts with each other, as well as bringing greater contact with the wider world. All of these things might be expected to have impact on how refugees perceive their present situation, how they imagine 'home', and how they characterise the relationship between the two.

'Transitional' dress and connections with home

Amongst those longer staying refugees who are not recently arrived from remote, traditional Kayah villages, some of the women's skirtcloths that are worn are traditional-style cloths made in the camps on continuous warp backstrap or non-automated frame looms. Several different kinds of such cloth are made in the camps, differentially characterised as 'traditional' to and by various Karenni groups. Other than the 'Karenni national' cloths (see chapter 3), the most common types are so-called 'Paku (Karen) and 'Padaung' cloths (Fig.5.5.i–iv). Both are predominantly black, with thin coloured stripes near the top and bottom of the skirt, and stripes and subtle patterning (warp *ikat*, in the case of the Paku cloth) in the central portion.

It is the weavers and wearers, not I, who characterise these two cloths as typically 'Padaung' and 'Paku'. Yet, this neat labelling does not necessarily fit with a complex ethnographic reality. 'Padaung' here refers to all Kayan, each of the self-defined subgroups of which actually has its own traditional cloths that do not correlate to the type described as 'Padaung' in the camps. Indeed, some of my Kayan friends said the cloths described as 'Padaung' were in fact typical only of Kayan Kang-nga in the Karenni State villages of Le-bah-hkoh and Lay-thoh-ya-dow, near Loikaw. Furthermore, the cloths are worn indiscriminately by both 'Padaung' and others (Fig.5.5.v).

Fig.5.5.iii

Woman's skirtcloth. 'Padaung' (Kayan), made in Karenni Refugee Camp 5, Thailand, by Oo Mey, and purchased in the camp from Naw Sarah, 1997. Cotton and polycotton, woven on a continuous warp backstrap loom. 1020 mm x 960 mm.
Royal Pavilion, Libraries & Museums WA508059, collected by Sandra Dudley

These cloths are worn particularly on Sundays (the refugee population is largely though by no means entirely, Christian), during festivals, and on other special occasions. Many women also wear these 'traditional', hand woven cloths on an everyday basis, especially in the cold season, as the cloths are thicker and warmer than the ubiquitous *batik*-printed polycotton sarongs. Nonetheless, these types of clothing are not worn daily by large numbers of people on the kind of scale on which recent arrivals in Camp 2 wear their traditional Kayah costume (see below). With the exception of so-called 'Paku' cloths, these cloths are also notable by their absence from early archive photographs and museum collections.

These cloths are, I argue, transitional in that they act as connections between the refugee camps and the present, and 'home' and the past.[4] To an extent, commercial *batik*-style cloths act similarly: because they are commercially available throughout Southeast Asia, refugees' ease of access to familiar cloths that are as easy to get now in Thailand, as in the past back home, provides a degree of continuity with the past. Similarly, the more traditional-style Paku and Padaung cloths now made in the camps were also made by women in the villages. In their presence and visibility in the camps, then, they too provide some sense of continuity, connecting in refugees' memories and imagination with the past and with the villages. It is with these traditional-style cloths that connection is greatest: it is not just their existence and availability in the camps that echoes experiences 'at home' in Karenni State, but also the formal occasions on which they are worn and thus their association with ritual continuity and tradition. Furthermore, their very production in the camps, using the same techniques as in the village-based past, also enhances a sense of continuity with that past.

Production of most cloth made in the camps involves women sitting either in or underneath their houses using backstrap looms. Refugees themselves often describe this method of manufacture as 'traditional', insofar as it is the method used by women in villages inside Karenni State. Refugee weavers or their husbands tend to make their own looms of bamboo and wood, usually using a piece of recycled rice sacking for the backstrap itself. Older women well used to weaving sometimes complain that the looms in the camps are not generally as good as those in the villages,[5] mainly because in the camps people have no cattle or other livestock from which they can obtain hide to make a strong backstrap after they have been slaughtered. Yarn is purchased ready-dyed from Mae Hong Son market or camp shops (which get most of their stock from Mae Hong Son market). In camps 3 and 5, for most women this is little different from village practice: unlike the new arrivals in Camp 2 (see below), most Karenni State women are not nowadays used to growing and preparing their own cotton.[6] For most women who weave in the camps and who learned to weave as girls in their villages, the activity of weaving is intrinsically bound up with their memories of 'home' and of the daily chores that were necessary there. In the camp, farming and free movement to market is not possible, but for these women weaving at least is one routine activity from the past that can be reassuringly continued in exile.

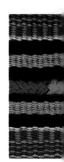

New refugees, traditional Kayah dress and connections with home

The post-1996 arrivals in Camp 2 are ethnically Kayah, the majority Karenni ethnic group. Most of the pre-existing Karenni refugee population is also Kayah. There are, however, some important differences. Unlike many of the pre-existing refugees, most recent arrivals cannot speak Burmese and in their villages had no access to health clinics or schools. Before crossing the border, most had apparently rarely, if ever, seen motor vehicles or foreigners. Their villages are remote,

Fig.5.5.iv top right

Naw Stand Htoo (name changed), weaving on a backstrap loom under her house, Karenni Refugee Camp 5, 1997. She is making a black and red/white strip, with warp ikat decoration at one side. This could become one half of a Paku Karen skirtcloth, but in this case the strip is being made to order for a Chiang Mai based non-governmental organisation, as part of an income generation project. This strip and others will be made up, in a workshop in Chiang Mai, into boxed jackets for sale abroad. Photograph by Sandra Dudley.

Fig.5.5.v below right

Naw Sarah weaving at a backstrap loom in her house, Karenni Refugee Camp 5, Thailand, 1997. She is making an unmarried girl's dress (now in the Pitt Rivers Museum, University of Oxford). She is herself Paku Karen, and she wears a Paku Karen blouse and a 'Padaung' skirtcloth.
Photograph by Sandra Dudley.

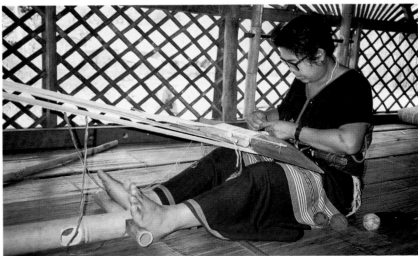

permanent hill settlements sustained by subsistence agriculture. Most have not converted to Christianity and instead practise traditional Kayah religion. Unlike longer-staying refugees, they also tend to have little conception of a pan-Karenni nationalism. Furthermore, many of the women in particular had not previously seen other Kayah women, such as those among the longer-staying refugees, who do not dress as traditionally as they do.

In their own eyes as well as in those of pre-existing refugees, recent arrivals are 'traditional' Kayah who 'continue to do as our grandmothers and grandfathers did'. For insiders and outsiders alike, the most obvious emblem of this 'traditional' identity is women's clothing. Almost all pre-existing Karenni refugee women wear a mid-calf length *longyi* and T-shirt or traditional tunic, and consider it improper to show any leg above mid-calf or the chest area (except when breastfeeding). All recently arrived 'traditional' Kayah women, on the other hand, wear now or wore on arrival an outfit in which the knees and lower thighs are exposed. This includes a skirtcloth and headcloth (Fig.5.5.vi), both of which are invariably home-made on continuous warp backstrap looms, using home-grown cotton coloured with

Fig.5.5.vi

Recently arrived, traditionally dressed Kayah refugee women, Karenni Refugee Camp 2, Thailand, 1996.
Photograph by Richard Than Tha.

vegetable dyes. The breastcloth, however, is usually made of commercial fabric, as may be the undyed fabric belt-cum-purse. Worn with these textiles are a string of old silver coins used as a belt, sash or necklace; necklaces of glass beads; large silver ear plugs and pendants; and a great number of black, lacquered, two-ply cotton rings worn around and just below the knee (Fig.5.5.vii). With the occasional exception of the headcloth, this full outfit is worn at all times, including at night. The silver is not only ornament, but also family wealth and heirloom for safe-keeping and passing on to the next generation. Archive photographs and early descriptions by missionaries, colonial officers and others indicate that this kind of costume has indeed been the customary dress of Kayah women for a long time, and certainly for much longer than the so-called 'national costume' favoured in the camps.[7]

A traditionally dressed Kayah woman sees this costume as an extension of herself, marking her not only as Kayah but also, through ear pendants, as a woman of certain age and marital status. However, the circumstances in which they had to leave home meant that few women could bring with them spare clothes and/or

Fig.5.5.vii

Recently arrived, traditionally dressed Kayah refugee woman and child, Karenni Refugee Camp 2, Thailand, 1996.
Photograph by Richard Than Tha.

cotton with which to make more. They had only the clothes they wore and, once those clothes became too worn or dirty in the camp the only alternative was to wear the ubiquitous sarong and T-shirt, a distressing prospect for new refugees.

But this dress is more than simply an expression of the wearer's identity. Immediately on arrival in the camps, traditional dress, an obvious marker of distinction in a situation of sudden exposure to people who looked different, was the only visible evidence of what and who the new arrivals were and had been. All of them, of either sex and whatever age, desperately hoped women would be able to continue wearing traditional clothes but were worried this would become impossible in exile, without cotton or the money to buy it.

Fig.5.5.viii

Two senior women and a young girl leaving the sacred pole area, having made an offering on behalf of all the women of the 'village', on the main day of the ka-thow-bòw festival in sections 5 & 6 of Karenni Refugee Camp 2, Thailand, 1998. In the foreground to the right is the main ka-thow-bòw pole, tied with offerings of chicken femurs. To its left, is a smaller offering platform bearing leaf parcels of rice and other food. Photograph by Sandra Dudley.

These anxieties were also due to dress becoming a focus for wider stresses resulting from exile. In part, this was because the *production* of traditional textiles is as important as the textiles themselves: the process of weaving, like the process of farming and the annual *ka-thow-bòw* festival (Fig.5.5.viii), is as important to the integrity of Kayah culture and as intrinsic to being Kayah, as are the end-products. Suddenly being unable either to weave or farm, was a stressful experience that exacerbated the trauma of violent displacement itself.

Weaving is simultaneously connected to the past and 'home' – what has been left behind – and to the painful leaving-behind process itself. Like traditional festivals, it was one of the things refugees prioritised in their anxieties about making their new, exilic situation more familiar. Weaving itself and the clothing that results from it are both symbols of the past and important factors in trying to 'enculturate' the present with familiar activities and things, thus making it more bearable. Weaving and traditional Kayah dress simultaneously represent and continue the past, and act as reminders of it 'at home'. This is intrinsic to the process of becoming a refugee and of developing exilic anxieties and an exilic imagination of 'village' and 'home'. These imaginative and cognitive connections extend through time and space to tie a Karenni individual to the territory and identity of 'Karenni'.

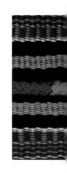

Chapter 6

Burma textiles in wider contexts: collecting, commissioning, research

6.1 Documenting Chin textiles

John Barker

When James Green visited the Chin Hills in the 1920s and '30s he collected nine weavings, described as 'blankets'; a striking photograph from a series he took illustrates their use (Fig.6.1.i).[1] This small number is typical of other early collections, largely because of the geographical inaccessibility of most Chin territories. In North America, only Denison University received a substantial number (152), donated by Baptist missionaries.

Detail: woman's tunic-top (kor). Haka, central Chin State. See Fig.6.1.iii.

Fig.6.1.i

'A group of Chin men'.

Photograph by James Henry Green, 1920s.

Royal Pavilion, Libraries & Museums A0123

In 1996, large quantities of red silk cloths and skirtcloths (Fig.4.3.i, Fig.6.1.) began appearing in shops in Thailand, soon followed by loincloths, short tunics (Fig.6.1.iii, Fig.6.1.iv), and other northern and then southern Burmese Chin textile types. None had attribution beyond 'perhaps Chin'. Such 'outflows' of older, unknown textiles have often occurred throughout Southeast Asia during the last 25 years. As commodities in commercial streams, they travel to varying destinations, assuming differing identities. Tourists or expatriates buy them as souvenir decorative art. Inexpensive or damaged weavings are incorporated into 'ethnic' garments. Unusual, representative, or particularly fine examples might join the holdings of dealers and collectors for placement into institutional or private collections. Here they may be viewed as artworks or as documents of culture or of textile history (or any combination of these).[2]

In most cases, little is done to field document the material before it is dispersed. This will certainly impede later research efforts and may also preclude the attribution of specific types of works to makers' groups and subgroups. Even if we view these textiles exclusively as artworks (or fine crafts), we still might wish through specific attribution to recognise the artistry and skill of particular groups of 'hill-tribe' weavers, especially considering the historically derogatory attitudes held towards their arts by outsiders.

Fig.6.1.ii

Woman's skirtcloth (hnitial). Haka, central
Chin State. Silk; warp-faced tabby ground with
discontinuous supplementary weft patterning.
Detail of skirtcloth on page 58.
1260 mm x 860 mm.
Royal Pavilion, Libraries & Museums
WA508258

In my initial research efforts, I learned how little had been written on Chin weavings.[3] Early, colonial period accounts and two later anthropological studies provide some contextual information, a number of images, and several direct references,[4] but no material culture surveys or studies of Chin textiles *per se* were undertaken. Most fieldwork opportunities had ended in the early 1960s and all but a few Chin territories have remained closed to foreign visitors until the present. No reliable information was forthcoming from commercial sources. These older, distinctively patterned weavings clearly deserved to be properly attributed and documented, but how to proceed?

An unusual opportunity arose when I met an extended Chin family in Burma who offered to help document these mysterious textiles. Their language and cultural expertise were self-evident. Extensive family, church and business contacts afforded access to most Chin regions. I hoped that by joining forces we could make a useful contribution.

Without formal training in textile research, and given many logistical obstacles, I chose a purely 'documentary' approach. The main goals have been to accurately attribute selected types to makers' groups, to record local names used for them and to identify the range of related, finely patterned textiles produced within each group. Much other information is also emerging in the process. We note and assess this for future possible research applications.

Fig.6.1.iii *above*
Woman's tunic-top (kor). Haka, central Chin
State. Silk; warp-faced tabby ground, twill
weave, discontinuous supplementary weft
patterning. 550 mm x 415 mm.
Royal Pavilion, Libraries & Museums
WA508257

Fig.6.1.iv *right*
'Two Haka girls'.
Photograph by James Henry Green, 1920s.
Royal Pavilion, Libraries & Museums 0548

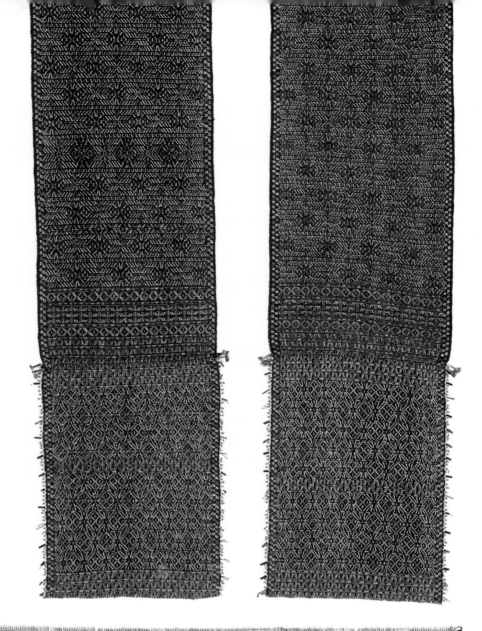

Fig.6.1.v right

Detail of man's loincloth (daun or deri enat). Mru Arang, northwest Rakhaing State. Cotton, silk, glass and plastic beads; warp-faced tabby ground with multiple supplementary weft weaves. 3980 mm x 140 mm.

Hollander collection

Fig.6.1.vi below

Breastcover (marankite). Mru Arang, northwest Rakhaing State. Cotton, silk, glass and plastic beads; warp-faced tabby ground with multiple supplementary weft weaves. 680 mm x 340 mm.

Hollander collection

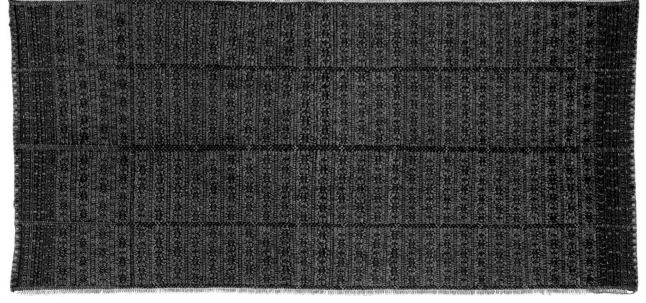

The main method employed has been for young Chin 'surveyors' (equipped with cameras and notebooks) to make 10 to 25 day visits into textile producing areas. They locate older weavers, explain the aim is to document and make better known their wonderful textiles, photograph weavers and ideally textiles if permitted, note the women's names and ages, and ask a series of open questions about the textiles. A second effort involves locating and interviewing older members of Chin subgroups living in Rangoon. A third component is interviewing a knowledgeable source in Rangoon who has lived in many parts of Chin State and has a broad familiarity with these textiles.

None of this has been straightforward, but the circumstances require experimental approaches and the results to date have been encouraging. A major hurdle was clarifying ethnic terms (see also chapter 3). This is quite a Pandora's box: each subgroup has at least two competing names, usually each with various spellings. Most were outsider-imposed, some are derogatory, and the term 'Chin' itself is controversial.[5]

Fig.6.1.vii

Detail of woman's headcloth (ta po lai).
Lauktu, Ann township, Rakhaing State.
Cotton, silk, trade pompoms; warp-faced
tabby ground with multiple supplementary
weft weaves.
1920 mm x 510 mm.
Hollander collection

Khami, Khumi and Mro textiles are central to my efforts, but have presented vexing attribution issues. Complex patterns of migration and intermarriage among these groups have produced a confusing assortment of ethnic terms. A visitor in 1921 noted intermingled groups of Khami and Mro inhabiting one river valley. He wrote 'the Kami [sic] are of two kinds, the Ayaing and the Awa' and that between them 'there is a certain degree of difference with regard to modes, manners and religious beliefs'. Of the more remote upriver Ayaing groups he noted that 'some of the Mros are taking the Kami (Ayaing) to [sic] wives and talking the language of their wives; while the Kami (Awa) have not done so'.[6] Given this situation, it is not surprising that a number of varied textile types of hybrid styles have emerged from these peoples and areas. The Mro loincloth and breastcover of Fig.6.1.v and Fig.6.1.vi are just two examples; these resemble their Khami counterparts in dimensions and general use, but display very different patterning.

Our first survey, in 2001, addressed Laytu and Sungtu textiles and served as a trial. A second survey in 2002 involved visiting Khami and Mro, then Sungtu, Laytu and Asho peoples. A relatively unknown group, the Lauktu, was also found and documented. Their distinctive textiles include a patterned long tunic and the resplendent silk headcloth in Fig.6.1.vii. In all, fourteen 'new' types have been identified from among these groups. In the north, a long survey in Falam and Haka townships has begun documentation of the red silk and indigo cotton traditions illustrated, as well as other related types. In both areas, we have begun to identify specific textile uses and gain some historical insights. We are accumulating information on materials used in dyeing and weaving. For some textiles, design names and their possible meanings are also coming to light.

These research efforts have been paralleled by the collecting and documenting of these textiles. The goal here is to transform a purely commodity-supply network into one that also provides useful information. It is a difficult adaptation, but has brought some useful results to date. In summary, our goals are being met and more is expected in the future as field methods and skills improve. Planned future research will also include the current production of certain Chin textiles for new markets.

Returning to the earlier discussion of 'outflows' and 'destinations' of works like these, the sale of older traditional textiles results from many circumstances besides the existence of outside markets. Accelerating cultural transformations, economic hardship in some areas, the importation of new and cheap trade garments and changing fashions among younger generations, all play a role. Documentation, research and publication, conducted with the involvement of local researchers who gather cultural, technical and historical information, can help to reveal, record and enrich everyone's appreciation of these superb Chin textiles, old and new, and of their makers.

6.2 Collecting Shan textiles and their stories

Lisa Maddigan

James Green collected over 50 Shan textiles while he was in Burma. His collection ranges from men's everyday cotton trousers and shirts, to gowns made with imported Chinese silk brocades and ornate appliquéd skirtcloths (Fig.6.2.i). Some of the textiles may have been collected as part of his anthropological work, some were gifts or souvenirs (see Fig.2.xv, page 27). Unfortunately Green did not record the stories that would either link them to his own work and experiences in the Shan states, or personalise them in relation to their makers or wearers.

Interest in the collection at Brighton has inspired others to add their textiles to those collected by Green. Recently acquired Shan textiles include nineteenth and early twentieth century outfits brought to England by people who lived or worked in Burma. The Green Centre has been working to ensure that the stories and memories surrounding these textiles are recorded.

Shan textiles brought from Burma by Eleanor Gaudoin (Sao Nang Sum Pu) and Sao Hkam Hip Hpa (Ivan) are heirlooms that for them evoke powerful memories of their family life based around the Shan Court at Hsenwi in the early to mid twentieth century. A dress worn by a nineteenth century Shan woman of status, collected by William Nisbett was donated to the Museum by his granddaughter, Janet Browne. Nisbett played a part in the early stages of Britain's exploration and administration of northern Burma, and it is likely that he kept textiles as souvenirs or records of what were for him unfamiliar places and people. All three collections present interesting comparisons with Green's own collection of Shan textiles, introducing very different but interwoven experiences of the Shan states in an era when the British colonial administration was developing its presence and influence in northern Burma.

Detail: woman's skirt. Shan, collected during the 1880s. See Fig.4.7.v, page 91.

Eleanor Gaudoin collection

Eleanor Gaudoin lives in Brighton. When she saw a Shan skirt collected by Green exhibited in the Museum, it brought back memories of her childhood as the daughter of a Shan princess. Eleanor discovered there was a letter and dictionary written by her father in Green's archive,[1] and donated her own collection of Shan textiles to the Museum in 1993. The textiles have inspired a series of oral history recordings, building a vivid picture of Eleanor's experiences of growing up in northern Burma.[2]

Fig.6.2.i *left*

Woman's skirt. Shan, northern Shan State, made during the early 20th century. Black cotton skirt, with two bands of black velvet attached toward the base. Decorated with a broad, 330 mm appliqué band toward the base of the cloth. Appliqué consists of alternating bands of heavily embroidered floral motifs on silk, and geometric supplementary weft panels.
890 mm x 817 mm.
Royal Pavilion, Libraries & Museums
G000031

Fig.6.2.ii *right*

Sao Hseng U, Golden Palace, Hsenwi, c.1932. Photograph copyright of Eleanor Gaudoin.

Eleanor's maternal grandfather, Hkung Hsang Tong Hung, was the Sawbwa, or ruling prince, of North Hsenwi from 1888–1916. North Hsenwi was one of the semi-autonomous principalities that made up the Shan states of northern Burma. During the colonial period, Britain made agreements with the Sawbwas, establishing a system of indirect rule over the Shan states. The first major expedition into Shan territory left in 1887; by the 1930s and '40s when Eleanor was growing up, British presence was well established. Eleanor's father, E. T. D. Gaudoin, had joined the Burma Frontier Service from India, and was stationed at Kutkai, the nearest British post to Hsenwi. In 1920, he married Eleanor's mother, Sao Hseng U, daughter of Sawbwa Hkung Hsang Tong Hung and his first wife Nang Ywe. Eleanor's parents lived in various parts of northern Burma while she was growing up, but continued to pay frequent visits to her mother's family at Hsenwi.

Fig.6.2.iii

*Woman's skirt. Shan, northern Shan State,
made during the 1920s. Skirt incorporates
silk skirtcloth from northern Shan State, with
overlay of European imported gilt lace fabric.
980 mm x 640 mm.*

*"She wore this one when they were
entertaining or going to big parties. Because
she was married to a British administrator
my mother's social life wasn't really a Shan
social life … it was very European."*
Eleanor Gaudoin, 2000.
*Royal Pavilion, Libraries & Museums
WA507049, donated by Eleanor Gaudoin*

A jacket and two of the skirtcloths that Eleanor has donated to the Museum
originally belonged to her grandmother and her mother. Her grandmother bought
the purple silk brocade jacket more than 100 years ago from Chinese traders
who regularly came to the royal palace at Hsenwi (Fig.6.2.v). Eleanor remembers
her grandmother wearing a similar Chinese jacket during the winter months, but
with a fur lining and gold fastenings. For Nang Ywe, Eleanor's grandmother, this
style of jacket was everyday wear, but outside the court most Shan people wore
cotton, with silk only occasionally used for special occasions.

The silk and silver skirt was worn by Eleanor's mother in the 1920s (Fig.6.2.iii). The
gilt lace fabric is European, showing the early twentieth century vogue for
Art Deco style, and was ordered from a shop selling English goods in Rangoon.

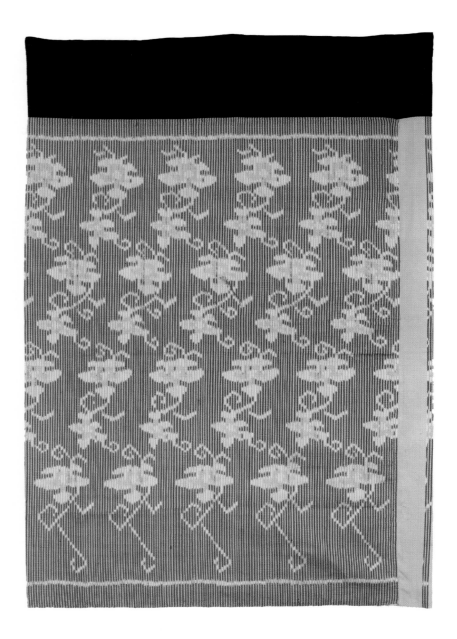

Fig.6.2.iv

Woman's skirt. Shan, northern Shan State, made during the 1920s. Silk skirtcloth with floral weft ikat patterns and warp stripes. 1060 mm x 835 mm.

Royal Pavilion, Libraries & Museums WA507051, donated by Eleanor Gaudoin

It was made up into a Shan style skirt tube using a vivid silk skirtcloth with a black cotton waistband, as a lining. It was not uncommon for European fabrics to be incorporated into more traditional costumes by Shan high society.[3] Eleanor's mother gave her this skirt when she was sixteen, and she has worn it many times since.

Eleanor donated four other skirtcloths to the Museum: three of her own silk cloths, and another that had belonged to her mother and is woven in silk with striking floral weft *ikat* patterns and yellow warp stripes (Fig.6.2.iv). Eleanor brought the textiles with her when she left Burma for England in 1958.

Fig.6.2.v

Woman's jacket. Purchased late 19th century in Hsenwi, from Chinese traders. Purple silk brocade. 520 mm x 1260 mm.
Royal Pavilion, Libraries and Museums WA507055, donated by Eleanor Gaudoin

Sao Hkam Hip Hpa collection

This gentleman is a Shan Prince, son of the ruling Prince of the State of North Hsenwi, and nephew of the President of Burma.
James Green 1948[4]

Eleanor Gaudoin introduced her cousin Sao Hkam Hip Hpa to the Green collection at Brighton. Sao Hkam Hip Hpa grew up in the palace complex at North Hsenwi. His family heirlooms include a silk brocade robe that he has loaned to Brighton Museum (Fig.6.2.vi). It belonged to his father Sao Hom Hpa, who ruled North Hsenwi from 1925 to 1959. Sao Hkam Hip Hpa has been living in England permanently since 1967, by which time the Shan states were under Burmese military rule and a perilous place for representatives of the former elite to remain.

The robe was tailor made for Sao Hom Hpa in Mandalay in the mid1920s, and originally had diamond buttons. It was worn for important state occasions with a fine silk suit, a plain silk turban and a silver chain of office bearing the North Hsenwi State dragon emblem. Sao Hkam Hip Hpa compared this front buttoned, knee length style of robe to those worn by Maharajas in India. He thought this influence might have stemmed from 1903, when a large party of Shan Sawbwas travelled to India to celebrate the coronation of King Edward VII at the Delhi Durbar, alongside other state rulers of Asian countries under British sovereignty. By the 1920s, it was a style often worn in Shan courts. It differs from the elaborate, sequinned, golden outfits that had been worn by previous generations of Sawbwas and that were strongly associated with the Burman court (see chapter 5).

Fig.6.2.vi

Man's robe. Silver and silk brocade.

Sao Hkam Hip Hpa collection

Fig.6.2.vii

Sao Hom Hpa on the throne in the Golden Palace at Hsenwi, 1935. Sao Hkam Hip Hpa, aged 8 at the time, is seated below him. James Green also photographed the elaborate throne on one of his visits to the Palace in the 1920s.

Photograph copyright of Sao Hkam Hip Hpa.

James Green was well acquainted with this influential Shan family, and visited the palace at Hsenwi on several occasions in the 1920s and '30s. When Sao Hkam Hip Hpa came to England to study in 1947, James Green became his guardian and in 1948 described Sao Hkam Hip Hpa's parents as 'personal friends of mine of long standing'.[5] Sao Hkam Hip Hpa and Eleanor Gaudoin's collections and memories of Hsenwi have greatly enriched the Green collection today, introducing personal and sentimental recollections of an area where Green worked. For both, the textiles, photographs and memories recall a magnificent era of Shan high society and courtly life that no longer exists. Sao Hkam Hip Hpa's father was the last Sawbwa of North Hsenwi.

Janet Browne collection

> I suspect that my grandfather deeply loved Burma, and he obviously collected a
> lot of things … your letter has made me unearth what family papers and
> photographs I do possess and I am going through them again.
> Janet Browne, 2001

The British Army posted William Nisbett to the frontier territories of Burma in the 1880s. After taking Mandalay in 1885, the British were keen to assert their influence in the neighbouring Shan states and organised various expeditions into the Shan hills. Nisbett made maps of the Shan states for the British Army and, like

Fig.6.2.viii

William Nisbett, photograph taken c.1895.
Photograph copyright of Janet Browne.

Green, took a keen interest in the people among whom he was living. He learnt to speak the Shan language, painted the people and places around him, and collected a number of artefacts, including a Shan woman's outfit (see skirtcloth Fig.4.7.v, page 91). The finely woven and appliquéd Shan skirtcloth and elegant silk jacket are complete with leggings, sandals and silver bracelets and would have been worn by a woman of high status. The outfit remains in excellent condition, suggesting that it has hardly been worn, if at all.

Janet Browne donated the outfit to the Museum in 1996, along with several Palaung and Burman items. The Museum has brought together dispersed records of Nisbett's experiences in Burma, adding photographs, copies of his paintings and a record of his military career to the documentation of his textile collection.

The parallels between Nisbett and Green are strong: both worked for the British Army in Burma, and both, like many colonial officials, had an interest in recording the appearance and culture of the people they met. This interest was driven by a climate of colonial exploration and discovery that swept the Shan hills of northern Burma from the late nineteenth century. Any personal memories and associations that the outfits might have had for Nisbett and Green have not been recorded, but Eleanor Gaudoin and Sao Hkam Hip Hpa's recollections show how interlinked the lives of colonial officials and Shan high society could be.

6.3.1 Making textiles in Myitkyina, 2001–2

Lisa Maddigan

In July 2001, the Green Centre commissioned weavers in Kachin State to make seventeen wedding outfits (Fig.6.3.1.i). Each outfit has been made to the highest standard and thoroughly documented with the weavers, including photographs and interviews recorded at different stages of the project. The commission developed out of a long-standing relationship with Kachin cultural history researchers who, since 1996, have contributed valuable contemporary insights to the photographs, documentation and textiles collected by James Green in the 1920s.[1]

The commission evolved over several months. The project co-ordinator in Myitkyina, Sadan Ja Ngai, consulted with weavers, researchers and members of cultural committees to define what would be a good representation of Kachin weaving.[2] The project was taken as an opportunity to record designs and techniques associated with traditional Kachin dress. This was seen by local people who were involved, both as something that would be of local value and as an appropriate way of representing Kachin weaving for a museum.[3] A selection of weavers in Myitkyina were commissioned to make male and female wedding outfits in what they considered to be the traditional style of dress for each of the six main Kachin groups – Rawang, Zaiwa, Lisu, Jinghpaw, Lhaovo: and La:cid, as well as outfits from two Jinghpaw subgroups with distinct styles of dress. In addition, a machine woven, tailored two piece woman's suit – a contemporary style of dress now commonly worn by Kachin brides at their wedding reception – was commissioned (Fig.6.3.1.iii).

Detail: man's bag. Kachin, Jinghpaw Hkahku,
made by Gwi Kai Nan in Myitkyina, 2002.
See Fig.6.3.1.iv.
Royal Pavilion, Libraries & Museums
WA508707

Fig.6.3.1.i *above*

Full group. Htoi Awng, a professional photographer in Myitkyina, took photographs of Kachin models wearing the completed outfits at the Manau festival ground in March 2002. Photograph by Htoi Awng.

Royal Pavilion, Libraries & Museums B0091

Fig.6.3.1.ii *right*

Man's jacket (palawng) and bag (n'hpye). Kachin La:cid, made by Maran Hka Tawm and U Thwin tailors in Myitkyina, 2002. Jacket woven in separate widths on a backstrap loom, using white cotton, with supplementary weft patterns in wool, and tailored to form a long jacket. Jacket 1380 mm x 1480 mm, bag 980 mm x 320 mm.

Royal Pavilion, Libraries & Museums WA508739, 40

Fig.6.3.1.iii

*Skirt and blouse (palawng). Kachin,
contemporary style wedding outfit for a
woman, made by Sa Tu Ja Lai in Myitkyina,
2002. Two-piece costume tailored from silk
fabric, with supplementary weft patterns.
Skirt 1030 mm x 440 mm,
blouse 560 mm x 980 mm.
Royal Pavilion, Libraries & Museums
WA508717, 18*

As a representation of Kachin weaving, the seventeen commissioned outfits are
selective, introducing the work and ideas of nine individual weavers working in
Myitkyina in 2002. Their choices of designs and techniques, and their descriptions
of the outfits in the documentation, have been influenced by the project's
emphasis on recording the 'most traditional' group styles, and by the association
with a foreign museum. However, the ways in which the weavers interpreted this,
their individual understanding and knowledge of traditional designs and
techniques, and their different approaches to weaving not only formed the focus
of the project but also resulted in a collection of highly individual outfits. The
Museum's involvement had significant impact, in other words, but the
documentation and selection of designs were also heavily influenced by local
contexts, changing definitions of group identity, and the ways that traditional dress
has been produced, used and defined in Kachin State over time (see Mandy
Sadan, chapter 6.3.2).

Fig.6.3.1.iv above

Bag. Kachin, Jinghpaw Hkahku, northern Kachin State and Hukawng Valley.
This bag, collected by Green during the 1920s, shows the same designs as those on an heirloom bag used by Hkahku weaver Gwi Kai Nan as her source for the new Museum commissioned bag in 2002 (see bag detail at head of chapter). Traditionally, the 'dragon motif' bag would only have been carried by a Kachin chief. The rare supplementary weft design is considered one of the most difficult to reproduce.
Royal Pavilion, Libraries & Museums G000003

The designs that the weavers chose to use vary from work meticulously copied from their own heirloom textiles, to pieces incorporating innovative new designs, materials and accessories. Some weavers based their choice of design on what they could remember their elders wearing, or on what they had been taught by their mothers and grandmothers (Fig.6.3.1.iv). For some outfits, this differed from what is worn today as 'traditional dress'. Muk Yin Haung Nan, who made the Lhaovo: outfits, paid particular attention to this, making two women's skirtcloths, one in the 'traditional' style worn today and one as she remembered them being made by her grandmother. Both skirts were woven on a backstrap loom, but the modern traditional skirt uses brighter colours and has many more patterns (Fig.6.3.1.v). Several of the weavers referred to an increase over time in the use of pattern, colour and silver decorations and most, although not all, designed their outfits according to contemporary interpretations of traditional style.

Fig.6.3.1.vi above

Woman's jacket (palawng the shatsawm jahtap). Kachin, Lhaovo: made by Muk Yin Haung Nam in Myitkyina, 2002. Tailored from black velvet, decorated with orchid fibre, sequins, silver and plastic beads. The weaver considers the yellow orchid fibre decoration to be a fundamental part of the traditional outfit, but said that it is often replaced with wool because the orchid fibres are so expensive to source. 485 mm x 1485 mm. Royal Pavilion, Libraries & Museums WA508762

Fig.6.3.1.v above left

Skirtcloth (labu). Kachin Lhaovo:, made by Muk Yin Haung Nam in Myitkyina, 2002. The weaver termed this a 'modern traditional style,' as opposed to the very different 'traditional style' worn in the past (see Fig.2.xix and Fig.2.xx). Woven in wool and cotton with supplementary weft patterns. 1120 mm x 840 mm. Royal Pavilion, Libraries & Museums WA508765

Particular attention was paid by many of the weavers to use what were considered to be the most traditional materials and techniques, for example home grown and hand spun cotton and silk, natural dyes, and specific seeds, fibres, buttons and coins for decoration. These methods often continue to be associated with high quality garments but are not always used because the materials are rare, and the techniques time consuming and expensive (see Fig.6.3.1.vi). Several of the weavers expressed their concern that knowledge of these materials and techniques is increasingly rare in Myitkyina, with fewer women learning the traditional methods of weaving, an increase in machine weaving and many weavers choosing to use cheaper and more readily available materials. This concern was a key factor in the choice made by people working on the project in Myitkyina to use the commission to record traditional Kachin methods and designs.

Making records in Myitkyina

The Museum views documentation as a critical part of this textile commission, and a way of continuing its broader concerns with Kachin archives and cultural records. The interviews and notes gathered by Sadan Ja Ngai and Salaw Zau Ring are an important record of approaches to weaving and weaving techniques, a field in which Jinghpaw language records are very scarce (Fig.6.3.1.viii). The interviews will be preserved as unedited recordings in Jinghpaw, and as written Jinghpaw summaries prepared by Sadan Ja Ngai. The summaries have been translated into English and are supplemented by notes from meetings between the Museum and the weavers in Myitkyina at the end of the project. In addition, summaries of Green's collection and background and of the Museum's current work and collecting policy, have been prepared by the Museum in English and translated into Jinghpaw for people working on the project in Myitkyina.

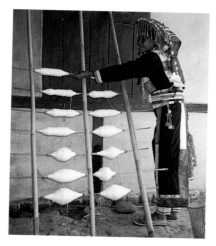

B0081

B0075

B0058

B0029

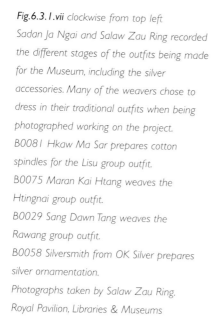

Fig.6.3.1.vii *clockwise from top left*
Sadan Ja Ngai and Salaw Zau Ring recorded
the different stages of the outfits being made
for the Museum, including the silver
accessories. Many of the weavers chose to
dress in their traditional outfits when being
photographed working on the project.
B0081 Hkaw Ma Sar prepares cotton
spindles for the Lisu group outfit.
B0075 Maran Kai Htang weaves the
Htingnai group outfit.
B0029 Sang Dawn Tang weaves the
Rawang group outfit.
B0058 Silversmith from OK Silver prepares
silver ornamentation.
Photographs taken by Salaw Zau Ring.
Royal Pavilion, Libraries & Museums

The project has encouraged dialogue about recording designs and techniques in Kachin State and it is hoped that this will continue. However, as with Green's own notes and photographs, it is crucial that the information gathered is viewed in context, and that it continues to be framed as the opinions of individual weavers, generated as part of a project initiated by the Museum.

Although the weavers and researchers were encouraged to choose their own designs and to structure the documentation themselves, the Museum's interests have had significant impact on what information has been recorded and on how the records have been constructed. Traditional culture, naming designs and their meanings, and the expression of group identity through dress are themes that feature strongly in the project. This relates specifically to the Museum's interests and approach to recording cultural traditions, and the interviews show that while some weavers work closely with these ideas, some had not directly considered their work in this way before. This mixed response has developed the Museum's understanding of how traditional textiles are made and perceived in Myitkyina, and at the same time highlights assumptions that were made about what the project should record.

Fig.6.3.1.viii

Man's jacket (palawng). Kachin Rawang, made by Sang Dawng Tang in Myitkyina, 2002. Made using handspun cotton and chemically dyed wool. Woven in strips on a backstrap loom, with tufted pile for extra warmth. Compare with Nung-Rawang cloth in Fig.2.ix and Fig.2.x. 700 mm x 1630 mm. Royal Pavilion, Libraries & Museums WA508791

The documentation of the project has also been influenced by the idea of building a resource that would be useful for people in Kachin State and for the Museum. The intention was to base this on recorded interviews with the weavers and to make transcriptions and written summaries of the progress of the project that could be translated into English. However, both the researchers and the weavers found making written records problematic.[4] This, and the complexities of transcription and translation, mean that in the process some details about weavers' backgrounds and how the textiles were made have been lost, and some have been generalised. This demonstrates the importance of reading the summaries as an integral part of the project and its processes.

The project has exposed a number of unanticipated issues about the Museum's focus on both commissioning work and documentation from within communities, and on building shared archives. Nonetheless, just as Green's collection serves as an important record of Kachin dress in the 1920s, and his notes and photographs are products of their time, the material gathered for the Kachin textile project, when seen in context, provides a valuable insight into textile production in Myitkyina.

6.3.2 Textile contexts in Kachin State

Mandy Sadan

In recent years, much importance has been attached by Kachin nationalists to the contention that Kachin identity is composed of six ethnic communities. This idea has been consolidated by the nationalist movement, headed by the Kachin Independence Army (KIA), since the outbreak of conflict with the government of Burma in 1961. It also reflects continued efforts to identify official numbers of ethnicities in Burma since the early nineteenth century.[1]

Since the signing of a cease-fire between the government and the KIA in 1994, there have been demands to identify a greater number of Kachin sub groups. This is a potentially divisive subject locally, but the ability of any group to present a distinctive 'traditional' style of dress is deemed of significance in such claims. Additionally, following the cease-fire, a number of Culture and Literature Committees have been established, which claim the right to protect the interests and cultural representation of the various subgroups. These Committees have had some impact on the standardisation of 'type' in costume design, especially through their claims that certain aspects of dress are distinctively and originally those of one community and not of another.

These, then, were some of the important local contexts that the co-ordinators and weavers had to negotiate in developing the recent project – deciding what was meant by 'Kachin' and how each part of the project added meaning to that term, whilst at the same time ensuring that the commissions did not become points of conflict in the community.

Detail: man's skirtcloth. Kachin, Jinghpaw Hkahku, made by Gwi Kai Nan in Myitkyina, 2002. Handspun silk. 1090 mm x 985 mm. This plaid design is instantly recognisable by people thoughout Burma as being 'Kachin'. Royal Pavilion, Libraries and Museums WA508704

Fig.6.3.2.i

*'My Head Quarter Staffs in the Shan States.
Labya La my Kachin orderly with bag and
dah, Subedar Sau Ohn, and a Kachin
policeman.'*

*The bag worn by Labya La on the left of this
picture is typical of that which became
known as a 'Soldier's Bag'. It bears a striking
resemblance to the bag described as
'Htingnai' in the recent project (Fig.6.3.2.ii).
Htingnai is a Jinghpaw geographical term for
the lowland area of southern Kachin State,
particularly those parts in close proximity to
the railway line and the Irrawaddy river.
However, few of the soldiers enlisted in the
Indian Army were actually from this region.
The Htingnai man's bag is considered one of
the most difficult of all Kachin men's bags to
weave (See also Fig.4.4.iv, page 72).
Photograph by James Henry Green, 1920s.
Royal Pavilion, Libraries and Museums 0761*

Contemporary concerns over how the identity
arise partly from the fact that, historically, the te
local people identify the important social relatic
multi-group identity, and the terms of reference
are uncertain, but it was certainly well establishe
political circles by the time the British administr
Initially transcribed in Roman script as *Kakhyen*,
in the mid 1830s through Burmese and Shan tr
vaguely defined (predominantly Jinghpaw) hill dv
region, which had a sometimes difficult relations

The implicit meanings of 'Kahkyen/Kachin' as a p
changed by usage in the British colonial state (I
administration was keen to interpret these high
terms of race, and ambivalence in ethnic/racial c
accommodated – maps needed to be 'fact', pec
administrative units. The term 'Kachin' was conso
Kachin Hills Regulation was introduced.[4] Over t
series of appendages to the label Kachin were i
established as its principal subgroups.[5] These ini
the region's socio-political structure acquired by
and missionaries, and were intended to help the
ethno-political administrative structure. Followir
Burmese state continued to utilise its power to
identity, advancing some and downplaying other
over 'nationality minorities'. Rarely did such labe
inter-group relationships on the ground.

Fig.6.3.2.ii

Bag (n'hpye). Kachin, Jinghpaw Htingnai,
woven and stitched by Maran Kai Htang in
Myitkyina, 2002. Wool, cotton, synthetic
ribbons, seeds, plastic beads and
silver disks / chains.
Royal Pavilion, Libraries and Museums
WA508669

Some of the convolutions of state structuring of Kachin ethnicity might best be understood by conjecturing what a 'Kachin Textile Project' might have produced and which labels it might have used, had it been commissioned at different points in this history. For example, if commissioned in 1830, the project might not have had much success at all. Objected to strongly by the groups to whom the term 'Kachin' was applied, those groups with whom the British authorities had closest contact preferred to use the term 'Singpho', which was a variant pronunciation of 'Jinghpaw'.[6] 'Singpho' was an identity ascribed to those Jinghpaw communities living in the Hukawng Valley region and westwards towards Upper Assam.[7] By the 1850s, these communities were artificially separated from the groups identified as Kachin by restrictions placed on cross-border traffic and by the enclaving of Singpho lands in the new Assamese tea gardens.[8] 'Kachin' thenceforward was consolidated as a Burma oriented ethnicity, from which 'Singpho' was excluded and confined to the state of India.

By the early 1880s, 'Kachin' was in common parlance among administrators and missionaries in the region, but it reflected the highly partial and politicised nature of contact that occurred among the peoples of this region.[9] A project at this time may well have privileged costumes labelled 'Gauri' or 'Atsi-Lahpai', as colonial contact was during this period confined to a relatively limited area around Bhamo, where these groups were most readily contacted.

If commissioned in 1955, a costume labelled 'Kachin-Naga' might have been included. In this year, the new administrative unit of North Hukawng in the Myitkyina District was created. Naga peoples, having strong links with neighbouring Jinghpaw communities, were now to be known as 'Kachin-Nagas'. The appellation did not stick, but again demonstrates the malleability of ethnicities in the political sphere.[10] Finally, if the project had been commissioned in the 1960s, it is possible that more importance would have been attached to incorporating a range of Lisu costumes. At this time, concerted efforts were being made to persuade Lisu migrants from China, who had crossed over into Kachin State following the Cultural Revolution, to affiliate themselves with the term 'Kachin'. 'Kachin' was not an official ethnic identity within China itself.

At all of these instances, the details of the costumes to represent 'type' would have differed – most noticeably, perhaps, in the increasing use of silver ornamentation across all the groups, and the increase in the degree of complexity in the designs and, in some cases, the prevalence of vivid red as a background colour. All, too, would be 'authentic' and all would be 'traditional' according to the communities themselves, yet they would also be deemed 'modern' or innovative in some sense. What they would not have been, however, was a static representation of an unchanging and timeless ethnicity.

Interpretations of the 'traditional' and modernity have changed over time, and the military, the colonial structure of which Colonel Green was a part, helped create new contexts for these notions. A battalion of regular Kachin soldiers was founded as part of the Burma Rifles in 1919, which drew from Jinghpaw and

Fig.6.3.2.iii

'Three Burman men and a member of the Military Police.'

This photograph shows Burmese men wearing ordinary cotton skirt cloths tied in typical Burman fashion.

Photograph by James Henry Green, 1920s. Royal Pavilion, Libraries and Museums A0041

non-Jinghpaw recruiting fields in the Kachin hills and beyond.[11] Unlike its previous usages, the identity 'Kachin' was deemed by these local soldiers to carry some positive connotations. In the military sphere, it was seen as a multi-group category which incorporated notions of modernity, some western ideas of development, and which conferred status in relation to the wider political sphere.[12] A context for a common 'Kachin' male dress was also established through the development of standard Kachin military uniform. Items representing the transition to manhood in local communities, such as the possession of a distinctive sword and use by all of a particular style of soldier's bag, were incorporated into the uniform of the Kachin troops (Fig.6.3.2.i, Fig.6.3.2.ii and Fig.4.4.iv). These became recognisable signifiers of a male Kachin ethnicity in the state sphere, despite considerable diversity in dress among the civilian Kachin male population as a whole.[13]

Some of these soldiers went on to become local political figures, with burgeoning nationalist aspirations.[14] They had witnessed firsthand the political structuring at Burma's political centre in the lead up to independence, and understood the significance of ethnic classification in these developments. Some began to call for the standardisation of 'Kachin' costume in civilian as well as military life; some called for the technical development of Kachin textile production as a cultural and economic resource. Some soldiers also raised the issue that Kachin identity was being challenged by the common tendency to assimilate items of Burmese clothing.[15]

The political contexts of dress and ethnicity have developed further following decades of political conflict since 1948.[16] Kachin nationalists today bemoan apparent changes in the ethnic control of textile production in Myitkyina, the capital of Kachin State. Since the KIA progressively took control of the jade mines after the 1960s, the perception developed that most Kachin women abandoned

Fig.6.3.2.iv

'*Group of Hkahku Men with guns at Kawa Pang.*'

This photograph shows a group of Kachin men wearing Burmese cotton skirtcloths similar to those in Fig.6.3.2.iii, but tied in Kachin fashion, with the cloth raised higher towards the knee, falling lower at the front below the knot. This photograph has been a cause of some confusion for non-Kachin people in lower Burma who are unfamiliar with more subtle signifiers of 'Kachin' dress than those most typically seen in state representations. Some have attempted to interpret the picture as being of a group of farmers who must have got up in a rush and did not have time to dress properly. However, the photo is carefully staged and these Kachin elders have posed themselves for maximum effect. This kind of misinterpretation of dress contributes to stereotypes about Kachin people that they are 'uncivilised' and 'dirty', which the modernisation of Kachin costume has attempted to challenge.

Photograph by James Henry Green, 1920s. Royal Pavilion, Libraries and Museums P0005

their work in the small textile factories to work as porters for the jade trade. Consequently, most Kachin textile production is deemed to be in the hands of Burman weavers, who do not 'understand' Kachin designs and debase them as a result. At the height of conflict with the government, the KIA also introduced harsh punishments for those who wore their skirtcloths tied in Burmese style (Fig.6.3.2.iii and Fig.6.3.2.iv). They also prohibited the use of *manau* designs on women's skirtcloths. The *manau*, traditionally one of the highest animist rituals that could be performed by a chief, was a deeply evocative cultural symbol in Kachin society and had been successfully repositioned as a nationalist emblem.[17] This *manau* pattern apparently became popular very quickly after being incorporated into designs seen at Union Day celebrations (see below). However, the KIA believed that associating the *manau* with women's dress would reduce its potency as a martial symbol during conflict with government. This response reflected engendered attitudes to textiles seen elsewhere in Burma and beyond.

The post-colonial state's representation of ethnic diversity is also believed by many Kachin weavers to have had major impact on the development of Kachin textile design, especially in transformation of the 'traditional'.[18] Following independence, a state stage was needed upon which the ideal relationship of the state to its various minorities could be demonstrated. From 1952, the celebration of Union Day was assigned this role.[19] Union Day takes place on 12 February, the same day that the Panglong Agreement was signed in 1947. This was an agreement between Shan, Kachin, Chin and Burmese leaders, including General Aung San, that all would co-operate with the future Union of Burma government following independence.[20] Important in this agreement was a clause to permit the Shan States to secede after ten years, if so desired. Union Day, however, seems never to have celebrated the 'Panglong Agreement' *per se*, but instead the rhetoric of the 'Panglong Spirit', a spirit of federation rather than the actuality of one.[21]

Fig.6.3.2.v

Women's jackets (soi shakap na palawng chang). Kachin, made in Myitkyina, 2002, of black velvet, with silver soi by OK Silver. 460 mm x 1390 mm (arms extended). Top: Jinghpaw Hkahku. Middle: Jinghpaw Manmaw. Both made by U Thwin tailors. Bottom: Zaiwa, made by Lahpai Htu Raw. A group of Zaiwa elders insisted that the style of the soi used on this costume should be that which was common in Burma rather than that used on Zaiwa costumes in China. The Chinese Zaiwa design follows the across-the-chest style of jacket neck opening, commonly seen in China. Some of the weavers felt that this Chinese style was more beautiful than that seen in Burma, as the silver falls in a diagonal shape across the front, but the elders insisted on the Burma convention for Kachin soi.

Royal Pavilion, Libraries and Museums WA508710, WA508693, WA508785

Shortly after independence, the Shan States' right to secede was denied them and hopes of a federation subsequently vanished.[22] Transformation of the Panglong Agreement to a 'Panglong Spirit', however, enabled the State to insist on representation at the Union Day festivities of all officially recognised minority nationalities, even those such as the Karen who had not signed the Agreement. The Union Day festival, therefore, evolved a complex iconography of constructed political meanings and has been the main stage on which the state displays its ethnic diversity.[23]

Union Day celebrations then, as now, centred upon different ethnic groups performing dances in their respective 'traditional' dress.[24] On this stage, from many different perspectives it was easy to translate this as being their 'national dress', even though this might not be accurate. The costumes had to be presented as 'traditional' because the state needed to represent itself as defender of traditional culture and diversity. However, the Kachin representatives were aware of the widely held stereotypes that prevailed in lower Burma that Kachin and some other non-Burman people were backward, 'dirty' and uneducated (see Fig.6.3.2.iv caption). This kind of stereotyping had been significant in denying claims for the greater political autonomy of the Kachin region in the lead up to independence – Kachin people, it was said, were not 'advanced' enough to govern themselves.[25] The representation of dress that took place, therefore, was primarily a reflection of how these groups wished to be perceived by the Burmese State, and reflected new interpretations of modernity and traditionalism that were consciously designed for the occasion.

The people credited with having most impact on the development of Kachin textiles for presentation at Union Day were a group of Kachin loom owners from Myitkyina, of whom the most important were probably Htingbai La and Marip Ja Kan Gam. They introduced machine looms to Myitkyina in 1960–62, which coincided with the 'democracy era' in Burma, when Htingbai La was also a Member of Parliament. He was thus familiar with the representation of Kachin ethnicity at the Burmese centre and its implications in political debate.[26] It seems that it was these gentlemen's wives, especially Marip Ja Kan Gam's wife, who were responsible for preparing the dancing troupe to go to Rangoon every year and who designed their costumes.[27] The trend in Kachin ethnic representation was for increasing silver ornamentation as discs (soi) and other adornment sewn to the women's jackets, and was subsequently used on many of the women's costumes. Made principally by Shan *mongsa* blacksmiths, they were considered initially a striking feature of Bhamo area women's costume, but they soon acquired the status of a generically Kachin feature and are one of the signifiers by which non-Kachin people in Burma may readily identify a costume as being 'Kachin' (Fig.6.3.2.v, Fig.6.3.2.vi).

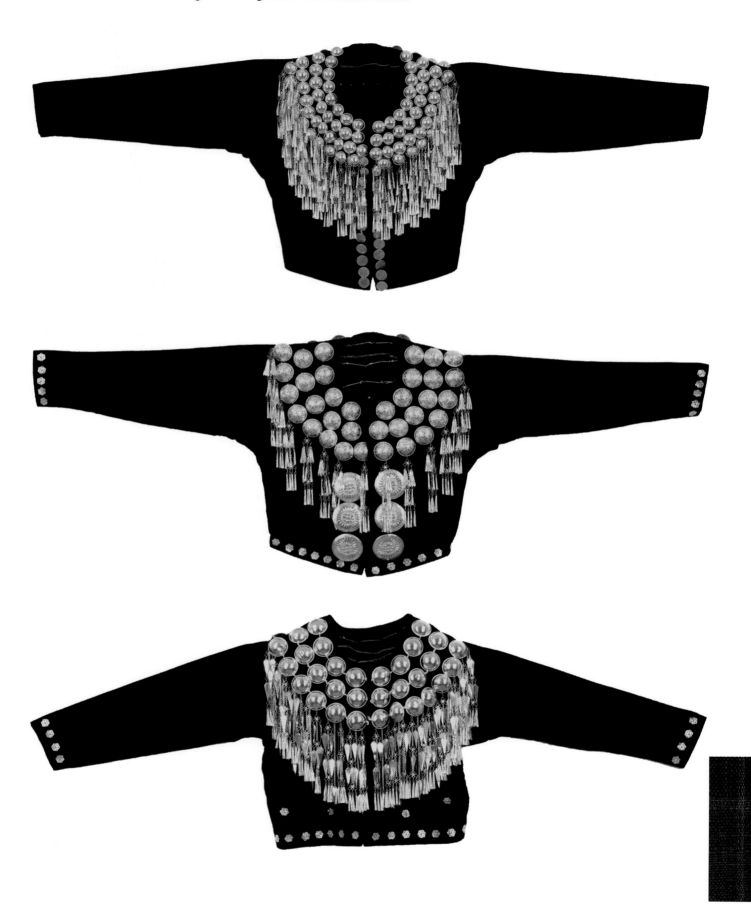

Fig.6.3.2.vi

Calendar, published in Myitkyina in 2002, incorporating photographs by James Henry Green. The Nung Lungmi Committee, which is attempting to gain official recognition as a Kachin subgroup, has developed a modern 'traditional' costume to represent their group. They have included small silver soi on the women's jacket as a reference to their desire to maintain a common Kachin identity. The Nung photographs in the James Henry Green Collection, however, demonstrate that in the 1920s it was most common for Nung girls to go topless. The new jacket is a way of incorporating notions of modernity, development and ethnic unity through dress – all of which are contemporary political concerns.

Royal Pavilion, Libraries and Museums WA508810

Increasing experimentation with colour and complexity in the woven designs arose from the designers' familiarity with the potential of machine loom weaving for elaboration. However, the looms that were used were foot operated, fly shuttle looms, and any backstrap loom weaver of adequate skill could thereafter replicate these patterns, if they wished. The new designs could then be absorbed back into 'traditional' weaving techniques. Htingbai La also experimented with the colours of male skirtcloths, and he is credited by some with popularising the

Fig.6.3.2.vii

'Two Palaung girls.' These Palaung girls wear jackets made of imported velveteen, adorned with silver. In some areas, such as the Kodaung Hill Tracts of Mong Mit, Palaung and Kachin communities lived in close proximity to each other.
Photograph by James Henry Green, 1920s.
Royal Pavilion, Libraries and Museums 1541

green and purple plaid design, which is again instantly recognisable by people throughout Burma as being 'Kachin' (see textile detail at head of chapter).[28]

Elaboration in the use of colour had been increasing since the later nineteenth century when imported dyes and dyed thread appear to have been increasingly popular among backstrap loom weavers.[29] However, this seems mainly to have taken place where Kachin women had access to the Shan five-day bazaar system.[30] In these areas, it was also easier to purchase imported cloth, and the use of black velveteen as the striking background to the silver *soi* seems to have developed from this contact (Fig.6.3.2.vii).

Attitudes to machine made cloth, elaboration in colour and design, demonstrate the complex range of contexts in which transformations of Kachin dress have taken place. The training required for setting up these looms was highly arithmetical, and obtained in the government textile schools in lower Burma.[31] This resulted in new gender roles as men were invariably chosen as technicians who set up the looms, whilst women translated their ideas to them and wove.[32] These developments helped frame the machine made cloth in terms of modernisation, educational achievement and consumerism. The new textiles were viewed as appealing purchases in some social and political contexts where transitions to 'modernity' were in focus. However, perceived changes in the ethnic control of the machine loom textile industry in Myitkyina, and the changing political contexts of ethnicity and dress brought about by three decades of conflict, have further complicated our interpretations of this context. Some women backstrap loom weavers have continued to resist incorporating the designs that have been created by machine, but many young Kachin women seem torn between their attraction towards more elaborately patterned and coloured clothing and their heightened aesthetic sense of what constitutes a 'real' Kachin design and what does not, which is invariably stigmatised as a 'Burman' error. However, few consider the quality of machine textiles to be as good as that produced by backstrap loom techniques. It is interesting that in the recent project, obtaining a good quality 'modern' tailored suit such as is frequently worn at wedding receptions became one of the most problematic commissions to resolve (Fig.6.3.1.iii).[33]

The textile project recently commissioned by the Green Centre has recognised the importance of context and incorporated this into the documentation and interpretation of the project. That the work has initiated debate in Myitkyina and in Brighton about the ways in which cultural heritage may be documented, preserved and developed is part of the results. It is hoped the project may enable local weavers and the museum to evolve new strategies for commissioning and labelling, and for developing locally relevant methodologies for collecting and interpreting items of dress and other textiles. This works towards gaining new, sensitive, collaborative and constructive understanding of dress and textile production in the Kachin region.

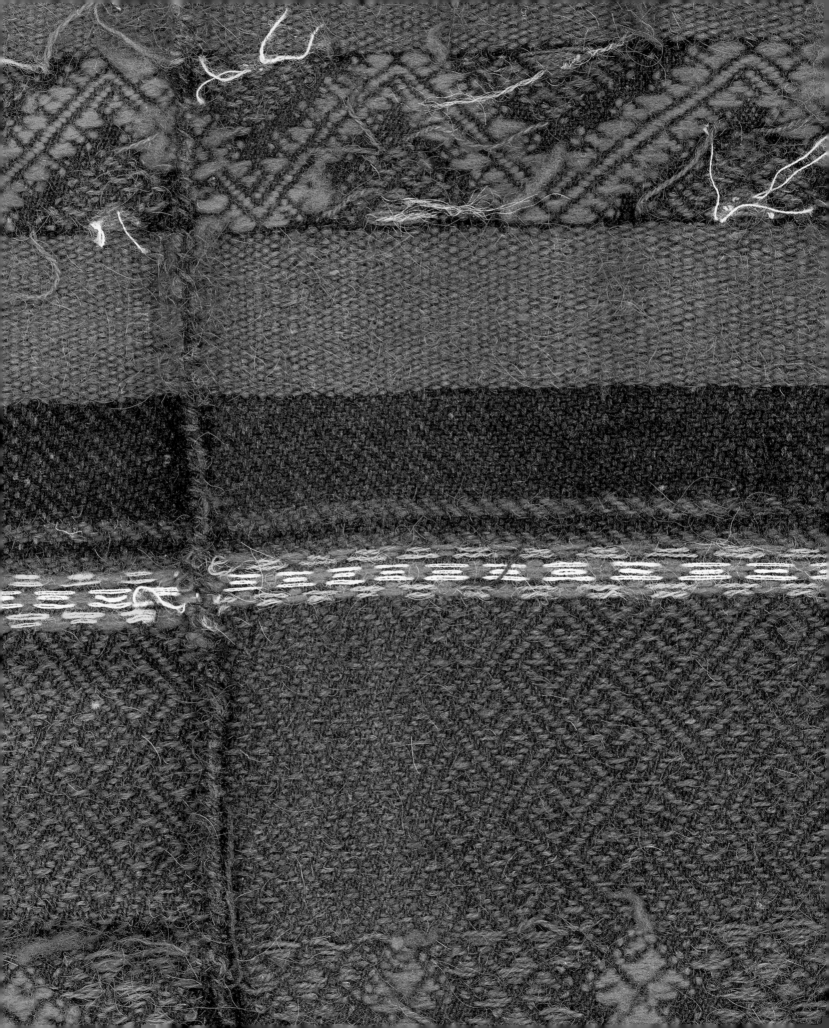

Appendix:
Museum collections of textiles from Burma

Sandra Dudley

This appendix lists some of the museums around the world that hold collections of textiles from Burma.[1] It is the result of a research project undertaken from June 1997 by the author into the distribution of textiles from Burma in international collections.[2] The list is not exhaustive, but comprises a valuable resource for further studies of textiles from Burma. They are based on a postal survey of 480 museums,[3] with follow-up visits to examine significant collections in Great Britain and North America.

The museums surveyed are in North America, Europe, Australia and New Zealand. For obvious historical reasons, concentrating on this area covered the major anthropological, colonial and missionary collections,[4] and a survey of such comprehensiveness had not previously been attempted. Nonetheless, this concentration entailed some significant omissions, particularly museums in Asia. There are many Asian museums of possible relevance, particularly in India, Thailand, China and Japan, as well as Burma itself,[5] but to do a comprehensive survey of this area would have been logistically impossible within the limited time and funds available.

What follows is a guide to what may be found where,[6] and to particularly significant collections. Collections might be deemed 'significant' because of:

- their size (e.g. Denison University)

- inclusion of items not well represented in other museum collections (e.g. Nottingham Museum in England and Indianapolis Museum of Fine Arts in North America both hold a

Skirtcloth (labu) — back detail. Kachin, Jinghpaw Sinli and Jinghpaw Gauri, southern Kachin State and northern Shan states, c.1900. 1630 mm x 630 mm.
Royal Pavilion, Libraries & Museums
G000022

number of interesting Chin textiles not found in many other, otherwise more significant, collections)

- inclusion of items of particular historical significance or particular geographical and/or ethnic strength (e.g. the George collection in the Bankfield Museum in Halifax, England, was made during the delineation of Burma's northeastern boundaries in the 1890s; furthermore, unlike many other collections it is strong in Palaung material)

- particularly good documentation and/or association with strong archive sources (e.g. the Green collections in Brighton and the Pitt Rivers Museum, England, are associated with good object documentation contemporary with Green [particularly at the Pitt Rivers Museum], with Green's diploma in ethnology [original in Cambridge], and with his extensive ethnographic photograph collection [Brighton])

It is, however, not only the museums listed below that hold textile items from Burma. Internationally, many institutions have just one or two pieces. *Kalaga* are often found: e.g. the Cheshire Military Museum, Chester, has two dating from the 1880s, and the Rijksmuseum in Amsterdam has another. Other museums have costumes or single clothing items: e.g. Guernsey Museum & Art Gallery has a Kachin woman's costume; the Art Gallery of South Australia has an *acheik luntaya*; Middlesbrough Art Gallery, England, has a Shan woman's costume from Panglong; the Russell-Cotes Art Gallery & Museum in Bournemouth has a single court or theatre costume; and the Bagshaw Museum in Batley, West Yorkshire, has three items from Burma, including an old Karen shirt. Many places have a shoulder bag or two (e.g. the Museum of Fine Arts in Houston), and some have other, textile-related items such as the two splendid lacquered yarn winders (one large and decorated) in Haslemere Educational Museum, Surrey.

Also important are photographic archive collections, usually colonial, missionary or anthropological in origin.[7] These are not listed below, although research of these archives can provide useful insight not only into textiles and clothing themselves, but also into how they were interpreted by the photographer, or how they connoted to both photographer and wearer, wider values and meanings. In particular, photographs often indicate a drive to 'type' people, and one of the main ways of doing this was by classifying groups according to their form of dress.[8] Significant archive collections of photographs include those at the Royal Anthropological Institute, the Pitt Rivers Museum,

the Royal Geographical Society, the Smithsonian Institution in Washington, D.C., and Green's photographic archive in Brighton, but many others of importance also exist.

Museums in Great Britain

- **James Green Centre for World Art, Brighton Museum & Art Gallery**
  Significant collection referred to throughout this volume. Especial strength is Kachin State material, including items being commissioned and made now

- **Eastern Art Department, Bristol City Museum & Art Gallery**
  Seven textile items, including a Shan woman's costume from Bhamo, and a weft *ikat* silk from Yaunghwe on Inle Lake

- **University Museum of Archaeology & Anthropology, Cambridge**
  Significant, large collection, including Shan, Kachin, Palaung, and Burman material. A particular strength is Namkham Shan textiles from Northern Shan State

- **National Museums of Scotland, Edinburgh**
  Sizeable collection, mostly late nineteenth to early twentieth century. Strengths include: some good, old Karen pieces (including items decorated with Job's tears and some lovely undyed garments with fine supplementary weft borders); wide range of everyday Burman and Inle Lake weft *ikat*

- **Art Gallery & Museum, Glasgow**
  Significant collection, mostly late nineteenth to early twentieth century, including Karen, Kachin, Shan and Burman. Also 30 modern cotton and silk *longyi* purchased in 1986

- **Hunterian Museum, Glasgow**
  Sizeable collection donated in 1966 by Mrs Leslie Langley. Most material is from northern Burma, particularly the Putao district. Strengths include: Jinghpaw, Nung and Shan

- **Bankfield Museum, Halifax**[9]
  Significant collection, mostly the George collection dating from the 1890s. Particularly strong in well-provenanced Palaung material. Also many fine Shan bags, some Maru bags and Kachin material, Taungyo garments, etc.

- **Leeds City Museum**
  Small but interesting collection, including a fine Pwo Karen shirt, and other Karen and Kachin items

- **National Museums & Galleries on Merseyside, Liverpool**
  Sizeable collection, mostly from the Imperial Institute and presumably mostly late nineteenth

century. Broad coverage includes Shan, Palaung, Kachin, Yao, Lisu, Lahu, Burman etc.

- **Department of Ethnography, British Museum, London**
  Significant collection, mid-nineteenth to late twentieth century. Strengths include: Lakher Chin and Khumi items donated by Lorrain in 1913 and 1928; other Chin material; Palaung; Karen

- **Horniman Museum, London**
  Sizeable collection but no information available

- **Victoria & Albert Museum, London**
  Large and important collection of Burman material and textiles from other groups. Main strength is mid- to late nineteenth century Burman and Inle Lake material, including court costumes (see Franklin, this volume), and a large number of *acheik luntaya* and weft *ikat* silks. Amongst other things, also has a good number of Karen and Shan pieces; Kachin items; and a few Palaung, Akha and Lisu costumes

- **Pitt Rivers Museum, University of Oxford**
  Significant collection, early nineteenth to early twentieth century, but also some late twentieth century items, including collection made by Sandra Dudley in Karenni refugee camps in Thailand. Strengths include: Nung and Maru items collected by Green; Khumi pieces; quilted, ornate velvet garments said to have been worn by 'King of Ava' (probably a Minister's clothes), collected in 1824; *sazigyo* collected by Richard Temple in 1889; painted cloths, both talismanic ones and a map; Karen clothing; Kachin bags; also a very important Naga collection (mostly from India)

- **Museum of Costume & Textiles, Nottingham**
  Thirteen items, including a good Inle Lake *zinme*, and four very fine Chin silks (supplementary weft)

- **Perth Museum & Art Gallery**
  Nine items, including *kalaga*

North American Museums

- **Phoebe Hearst Museum of Anthropology, University of California, Berkeley**
  Mostly Chin items from Tiddim, collected by the missionary Herbert Wehrly in 1958–60

- **Museum of Fine Arts, Boston**
  Ten items, including bags, Karen clothing (including items collected by Walter Bushell while a Baptist missionary, 1860–80), and a *sazigyo*

- **The Field Museum, Chicago**
  Around 40 Shan, Karen and other bags

- **Center for Burma Studies, Northern Illinois University, DeKalb, Illinois**
  Small assorted collection, mostly Burman and Kachin

- **Denison University, Granville, Ohio**
  Very large, important collection, mostly donated in the late 1960s and early 1970s, by ex-Baptist missionaries to Burma. Strengths include: Karen, Kayah and other Karenic groups, Akha, Lahu, Shan, Kachin Jinghpaw. Also some Chin material and a number of Inle Lake and Burman silks (including weft *ikat* and *acheik luntaya*). Some archive photographs too

- **Indianapolis Museum of Art**
  Twenty-eight items, mostly Burman (including *acheik luntaya*) and some very fine Chin pieces, including Khumi or Khami material

- **The Newark Museum, New Jersey**
  Some Karen items, and twelve fine Inle Lake, Burman and other silk *longyi*

- **Metropolitan Museum, New York**
  Four costumes, four bags and five other items; mostly mid-twentieth century; Lisu, Burman, Akha and Kachin

- **Royal Ontario Museum, Canada**
  Around 24 items, including Karen, Shan, Burman and Palaung material

- **University of Pennsylvania Museum of Archaeology & Anthropology, Philadelphia**
  Large collection. Strengths include: Shan, Palaung, *kalaga*; also an important Naga collection (India)

- **Smithsonian Institution, Washington, D.C.**
  Large collection, including missionary-collected material and two collections made in the 1960s by anthropologists (Brian Peacock & William Sturtevant). Strengths include: Inle Lake weft *ikat*; Karen, Pa-O, Hmong, Kachin and Lahu material

- **Peabody Museum of Archaeology & Ethnology, Harvard University, Cambridge, Massachusetts**
  About 80 items, particularly strong in Karen, Shan and Kachin material

- **Peabody Essex Museum, Salem, Massachusetts**
  Small but significant collection with some very fine nineteenth century Karen and Taungyo tunics, including items collected by the important missionary Adoniram Judson

European Museums excluding Great Britain

- **Museum der Kulturen, Basel, Switzerland**
  Sizeable collection, including Shan, Palaung, Kachin, Lahu, Bwe Karen, and Burman

- **Department of Social Anthropology, University of Bergen, Norway**
  Nine items, including a fine Karen tunic decorated with 'Job's tears'

- **Museum of Applied Arts, Budapest, Hungary**
  Seven clothing and textile items, mostly Burman, mid to late twentieth century

- **Danish Kunstindustrimuseum, Copenhagen, Denmark**
  Karen woman's tunic, and Shan bag, both decorated with 'Job's tears'

- **Stadtische Museen, Freiburg, Germany**
  No textiles *per se*, but a significant collection of clothed Burmese puppets, collected in 1908

- **Etnografiska Museet, Gothenburg, Sweden**
  Large and broad collection of non-Burman, ethnic textiles mostly collected by René Malaise, an entomologist, and his wife Ebba. Particular strength is Lisu. Also a sizeable archive photograph collection (mostly Malaise)[10]

- **Hamburgisches Museum für Völkerkunde, Hamburg, Germany**
  Over 30 items, the majority collected by an adventurer named Thomann. Includes Kachin Jinghpaw, Karen, Burman, Lisu and other material, including talismanic painted cloths and clothed puppets

- **National Museum of Finland, Helsinki, Finland**
  Four items only

- **State Museum of Oriental Art, Moscow, Russia**
  About 25 late twentieth century items, mostly Burman

- **Náprstek Museum of Asian, African and American Cultures, National Museum, Prague, Czech Republic**
  About twenty clothing and textile items, mostly Burman, mid to late twentieth century

- **Folkens Museum Etnografiska, Stockholm, Sweden**
  Over 30 textiles and textile-related items collected by René Malaise. Main strength is thirteen Pa-O items

Australasian Museums

- **National Gallery of Australia, Canberra**
  Around 24 items, mostly early and mid-twentieth century. Includes four *sazigyo*. Main strength is Karen material

- **Powerhouse Museum, Haymarket, NSW, Australia**
  Small collection of *kalaga*

Glossary

Acheik: Burmese. A group of distinctive tapestry weave designs based on wave and cable patterns; this term can also be applied to similar designs in wood-carving and lacquer.

Akhin: Khami Chin. A rectangular, breast-covering textile.

Achok-wun: Burmese. Court chamberlain in charge of tailors and seamstresses.

Appliqué: Decorative technique whereby pieces of fabric are applied (usually stitched) to the face of ground fabric.

Backstrap loom (body tension loom): A simple loom that uses the weaver's weight, leaning back, to maintain tension on the warp threads.

Bagyidaw: Burmese. Court artist.

Batik: A decorative dye-resist technique in which a substance impervious to the dye is applied, prior to dyeing, to the fabric, forming patterns.

Baung: Burmese. A high hat of crimson velvet decorated with applied gilt-foil ornaments; with a *wutlon* comprises Civil Court Dress.

Cashmilon: Mixed wool.

Cawng nak: A man's red, silk cloth (also referred to as 'blanket' by museums and others). Common to several northern Chin groups.

Cheulopang: Mara (Lakher). A high-status, northern Chin man's cloth, of indigo cotton with silk patterning. Similar cloths of the Haka are called *conlo* and of other northern groups, *tonlo*.

Chinthei: Burmese. A mythical lion; pairs guard the entrance to pagodas.

Cloth: As used in this volume, refers to a man's (sometimes a woman's) large blanket, mantle, or 'wrapper'.

Daun or **deri enat:** Khami Arang Chin. Loincloth.

Deh Xang: Akha. A village meeting ground where dancing, singing love songs and courtship take place.

Deva: A celestial being.

Double-faced weave: A warp-faced structure in which warp threads of two colours take complimentary paths so that one colour appears on the upper surface and the other on the under surface. Patterns arise by interchanging threads between the surfaces.

Dubhashi: Nagamese. 'One who speaks two languages'. Government interpreters.

Duyin thindaing: Burmese. Female state robe: green velvet robe, lined with yellow satin, with additional layers of breast, waist and neck ornaments in green, red and yellow velvet and satin, with gilt metal paillettes, metal purl and glass stones.[1]

Eingyi: Burmese. A blouse or jacket; worn by both sexes.

Gaonbura: Nagamese. 'Village elder', government-appointed chief of the village.

Ground weave: The weave employed in the main body of any textile.

Habune: Akha. A red textile used as a blanket.

Hintha: Burmese. An auspicious mythical bird, like a duck or goose.

Hkopeu-oki: Paku Karen. A woman's headcloth.

Hnitial: Haka Chin. A patterned red silk skirtcloth. Other northern Chin groups also use this textile type, but pronounce it *hni-tel*.

Hsei lat: Paku Karen. Woman's blouse.

Hse: Sgaw Karen. Tunic shirt.

Htamein: Burmese. A Burman woman's traditional wrap-around skirt; made in three sections, with a train.

Hti: Burmese. Umbrella; tiered, crown-like finial of a pagoda.

Ikat: A decorative resist process by which, prior to weaving, the threads of the weft (weft *ikat*) or warp (warp *ikat*), are placed on a frame to be tied and dyed in sequence according to the desired design.

Indigo: A natural blue dye derived from the leaves of the *indigofera* genus.

'Job's tears': *Coix lachrymi* seeds, used in decorating textiles.

Kachyi hkyengkalaga: Lisu. Woman's apron.

Kalaga: Burmese. Textile pictures, used as wall hangings. A velvet background (usually black) is decorated with embroidery, appliqué and padding, sequins and glass beads.

Kammavaca (Pali) or **Kammawasa** (Burmese): Manuscripts used for monastic ritual, most commonly for ordination.

Ka-thow-bòw: Kayah, Kayan, Kayaw, Manu-Manaw. The most important festival in the traditional annual cycle of all Karenni groups except the Paku Karen.

Gaung Baung: Burmese. A headcloth or turban for a Burman male; formerly self-tied, now ready-made.

Khran hain: Laytu Chin. A black or dark blue, short tunic with button-beads, of the northern Laytu Chin.

Khran in: Laytu Chin. A red, short tunic with white heart beads and cowrie shells.

Khreng tan: Sungtu Chin. A long tunic with magenta patterned band, beads and buttons.

Kinnara, Kinnari (Pali) or **Keinnaya, Keinnayi** (Burmese): Mythical half man, half bird creatures legendary for their loving devotion. They symbolise marital fidelity.

Konbaung: Burma's last dynasty (1752–1885).

Kor: A short tunic of red silk, worn by women of several northern Chin groups.

Kyizi: Burmese. A flat, triangular gong; emits a surging tone.

Labu: Zaiwa. Skirtcloth.

Lasi maka: Jinghpaw. Discontinuous supplementary weft.

Longyi: Burmese. A tubular sarong worn by both sexes.

Luntaya: Burmese. A tapestry weave technique: literally meaning 'woven with 100 shuttles' in reference to the many small shuttles filled with coloured thread used to create *acheik* wave and cable designs.

Luntaya acheik: Burmese. A tapestry weave technique used to create wave and cable designs on cloth.

Manau: Jinghpaw. Today, this is the main community festival celebrated by Kachin people and has become a symbol of ethnic unity and identity. It was originally a festival that could only be held by chiefs and was intended to bring blessings of prosperity and fertility upon the chief's family line.

Manuthiha (Burmese) or *Manussiha* (Pali): A mythical beast with the head and chest of a woman and twin lion bodies.

Marankite: Khami Arang Chin. A type of breastcover.

Mauk-yu: Burmese. A skull cap with ear and neck pieces; with *myindo myinshei* and *shweipei hkamauk*, comprises Military Court Dress.[2]

Mongsa: Jinghpaw. These people were traditionally considered a clan of Shan or Sino-Shan origin, and were respected as blacksmiths and talented silversmiths in Kachin State and northern Shan State.

Myindo myinshei: Burmese. A long-sleeved jacket (*myindo*) and skirt (*myinshei*) of imported velvet lined in silk with a deep border of gold brocade and silver spangled embroidery, with *ba-le-gwei* (gorget) and *chet-hpon* (breast plates) of overlapping pointed scallops thickly embroidered with silver-gilt sequins; with *mauk-yu* and *shweipei hkamauk*, comprises Military Court Dress.[3]

Myong: Akha. The leaves of *Polygonum tinctorium*, a low lying shrub, used to produce an indigo-coloured dye, but different from true indigo, *Indigofera tinctoria*.

Nat: Burmese. Spirit beings derived from pre- and para-Buddhist traditional beliefs; all require propitiation.

Navaratna: Sanskrit. Nine jewels, of cosmic significance since they represent the nine planets of Hindu mythology. The gems are: ruby, pearl, emerald, diamond, sapphire, coral, topaz, zircon and cat's eye. Arranged in a ring, eight are placed at points of the compass and the ninth in the centre. This is also the commonest arrangement in the woven 'block-ornaments' on *sazigyo*.

Neina: Khumi Chin. Beaded tubular skirtcloth, worn by women.

Ninaw or *niperthouk*: Paku Karen. Woman's skirtcloth.

Ne kouk: Khumi Chin. A narrow, beaded, rectangular breast-covering textile.

Nibbana (Pali) or *Nirvana* (Sanskrit): Cessation of individual existence. The state towards which Buddhists aspire.

Nyaungbin: Burmese. Sacred fig tree, *Ficus religiosa.*

Pada: Pali. Verse (or line) of four syllables, at least one of which rhymes with a syllable in the preceding and following verses.

Pahso: Burmese. A voluminous lower garment widely worn by the Burman male in Konbaung times. Worn as a sarong reaching to the ankles, with a large piece of spare cloth draped in folds down the front, or with the spare cloth passed through the legs and tucked into the waist at the back to form breeches.

Parabaik: Burmese. Book folded into accordion-like pages.

Pawa: Burmese. A shawl; a handkerchief; a breastcloth.

Phian: Asho Chin. A long tunic.

Puan lep: A fringed shawl used by women of several northern Chin groups.

Pyathat: Burmese. Many-tiered, spire-like roof.

Sadaik: Burmese. Chest for storing Burmese manuscripts; library.

Sanat maka: Jinghpaw. Continuous supplementary weft.

Sasana (Pali) or *Thathana* (Burmese): Religious teaching or dispensation.

Sazigyo: Burmese. Ribbons woven on a tablet loom for the binding of sacred manuscripts.

Sawbwa: Shan. Ruling prince of one of the semi-autonomous principalities that formerly made up the Shan states.

Shweipei hkamauk: Burmese. Gilded, brimmed, spired helmet; with *myindo myinshei* and *mauk-yu*, comprises Military Court Dress.[4]

Skirtcloth: Any textile worn as a kind of skirt or wrapper to cover lower body.

Soi: Jinghpaw. Silver discs that are sewn onto the jackets of some Kachin women's festive costume. They are sewn on individually, and although the effect may resemble that of a necklace, the discs are not connected to each other.

Supplementary weft: A group of related weaving techniques in which additional weft threads are introduced to the ground structure to create patterning.

Supplementary weft, continuous: A decorative weaving technique in which additional weft threads are continued back and forth across the entire width of the fabric.

Supplementary weft, discontinuous: A decorative weaving technique in which short, non-contiguous threads are introduced into

ground structure as weft-supplements, and woven back and forth across limited areas of the fabric only.

Tabby weave: The simplest weaving structure, also called plain weave.

Tablet loom/tablet weaving: In tablet weaving, warp threads are passed through the holes in the corners of flat cards or tablets. These are usually square so each tablet holds four threads. By giving a pack of these quarter-turns backwards or forwards, new sheds for the passage of the weft are created.

Tagundaing: Burmese. A flagstaff, usually topped with a mythical bird, at a monastery or pagoda.

Ta po lai: Lauktu Chin. Woman's headcloth.

Thadu (Burmese) or *Sadhu* (Pali): Literally, 'well done!' A formula used by witnesses to a deed of merit.

Tipitaka: Pali and Burmese. Literally, 'three baskets'; the Theravada Buddhist scriptures, made up of the Vinaya, Sutta and Abhidhama.

Tunic: Any sleeveless garment with 'V'-neck construction.

Twill weave: A weave in which wefts alternate over two warp threads and then under one warp thread.

Warp-faced: A weave in which weft threads are obscured in the ground structure.

Warp twining: A structure in which the warp threads from one tablet twine round each other forming a cord which encloses the weft. In Burmese *sazigyo*, this technique is used exclusively for the selvages (outside edges) of the tape.

Wutlon: Burmese. Long, kimono-style robe of velvet lined with silk with a deep border of gold brocade; with a *baung* comprises Civil Court Dress.

Weft-faced: A weave in which warp threads are obscured in the ground structure

Yetpya: Burmese. Braid.

Zardozi: Hindi, of Persian origin. Gold appliqué work (*zar* = gold; *dozi* = to lay upon).

Zinme: Burmese. Literally, 'Chiang Mai'. A distinctive weft *ikat* technique produced in the Inle Lake area.

Notes

Chapter 1
Introduction
Elizabeth Dell and Sandra Dudley

1   This volume with its starting point in the Green collections, chooses to use the term 'Burma' to refer to the country in which Green worked and collected, then governed by Britain as a province of India. Since 1989 the country has been known officially as 'Union of Myanmar', although this title is disputed in and outside the country. Other place names are also rendered as in Green's period, hence 'Rangoon' rather than Yangon and 'Irrawaddy' rather than Ayeyarwady, etc.
2   E.g. Fraser-Lu 1988 and 1994; Howard 1999.

Chapter 2
Green's collections and their historical and present contexts

James Henry Green, 1893–1975
Elizabeth Dell

1   See Dell 2000.
2   MS 1933, Green Centre archive, 'There is plenty of original work for a woman anthropologist, for so many important things cannot be investigated by a man'.

The Green collection at Brighton Museum
Elizabeth Dell

3   It is worth noting that the regional distribution is markedly different in Green's photographs and textiles – for example, while his Chin photographs are numerous and include examples of looms and weaving as well as documenting a great diversity of clothing, the Chin textile collection is very limited.

The Green collection at the Pitt Rivers Museum
Sandra Dudley

4   The name of this officer, or of another individual through whom he may have sent the Chin material to Green, is unclear on the extant letters in the Pitt Rivers Museum's related documents file. The signature looks like 'W. Biber', although no trace of such a man was found during extensive searches of colonial archives by Mandy Sadan. I am grateful to Mandy Sadan for this information, and for her suggestion that the letter writer may have been C.B. Orr (personal communications, 2000–01).

Green and textile collecting in the 1920s
Elizabeth Dell

5   See Green 1934, p. 250.
6   It was common for early ethnographic photographers, sometimes in the field or more commonly in their studios, to dress models from their own prop boxes, so that the same costumes reappear on a range of wearers. This does not appear to have been the case with Green, although he did literally 'compose' different people in front of the landscape backdrops. See Dell 2000, note 31.

Green, Oxford and anthropology
Sandra Dudley

7   See Odo and others in Dell 2000.

Chapter 3
Whose textiles and whose meanings?
Sandra Dudley

1   Parts of this chapter have previously appeared in Dudley 2000 and Dudley 2002.
2   The chapter is broad and cannot do full justice to what is a very complex area, but for further specific discussion of some of the sorts of issues it raises in a Kachin context, see Sadan, this volume. More broadly, see various in Eicher 1995.
3   C.f. Banks 1996.
4   C.f. Handler & Linnekin 1984. See also Barnes 1995.
5   Dudley 2000.
6   E.g. Scott & Hardiman's neat ethnic classifications (1900).
7   For further discussion of these issues in Kachin and Karenni contexts, see Sadan, this volume; Dudley 2000; Dudley 2002; Sadan 2000; Sadan 2002.
8   E.g. Dudley 2000 on others' glossing of 'the Karenni' as being sorts of 'Karen', despite (i) not all Karenni attributing similar meanings to 'Karen', and (ii) some not thinking of themselves as 'Karen' at all.
9   This includes Green's dissertation (1934). Nonetheless, it is important to note that Green was and is not alone in tying dress to identity – this is a phenomenon that is characteristic of most ethnography of Burma.
10   J. Barker, personal communication, 2002.
11   C.f. Odo 2000.
12   Wilson & Frederiksen 1995, p. 4; see also various in Barnes & Eicher 1992.
13   Ibid.
14   C.f. Hobsbawm 1983.
15   From an outsider's perspective, it could be said to be a 'Burmanisation' of traditional Kayah and other northern Karen styles of dress. Indeed, while in the field, on several occasions I referred to Karenni women's combination of skirtcloth and T-shirt/other upper garment, as 'Burmese-style dress'. To me at the time, this seemed convenient shorthand for non-traditional forms of Karenni dress, as some sort of upper garment teamed with a longyi reaching to mid-calf length does indeed comprise the usual mode of dress for women throughout contemporary Burma; furthermore, I meant 'Burmese' in a country-wide, rather than an ethnic, 'Burman' sense. However, for several reasons this was contentious from the point of view of my Karenni friends. It implied to them a lack of distinctiveness through inclusion in an apparently homogenous Burmese whole. For some of them, this was unacceptable on the grounds of political principle – for those conscious of Karenni National Progressive Party (KNPP; the self-styled 'government-in-exile' in the refugee camps) nationalist ideology, the description of their clothing as 'Burmese' in style implied incorporation within the Burmese nation-state, a notion against which many reacted strongly. But implications of inclusion within a Burmese whole were problematic for them on grounds of race as well as of political ideology, not least because they did not always distinguish as I did between 'Burmese' and 'Burman'.
16   Knauft 1997, p. 239. Transitional and national forms of dress could also be said to be 'symbolic inversion, on high days and holidays, which tells people what it is that they are in their ordinary daily lives ... [in which] they are, in their own eyes, "modern"' (Chapman 1995, p. 27).
17   Friedman 1992, p. 338.
18   C.f. Seng & Wass on Palestinian wedding dress in the USA (1995). The article points out that contrary to outsider understandings of 'tradition' as implying an unchanged form, 'the [insider] definition of what is traditional involves a selective process, for as long as an object contains

certain determined elements it may still be considered as "traditional". Both process and definition are dynamic' (*ibid*, pp. 229–30).

19   Macdonald 1997, p. 9.
20   Durham 1995, p. 189. See also Toren 1988.
21   Mai Aik Phone, personal communication, 1997.
22   Various informants, personal communications, 1996.
23   Dudley 2000.

Chapter 4
Textile traditions of Burma: a brief overview

4.1 Akha textiles
Mika Toyota

1   Goodman 1996, p. 72.
2   Lewis & Lewis 1984.

4.2 Burman textiles
Sylvia Fraser-Lu

1   Questions have been raised concerning this attribution, as surviving nineteenth century textiles from the Manipur area bear no relationship to *luntaya acheik* in design and patterning techniques. Contacts with the Chinese, noted for prowess in tapestry weaving techniques, have also been suggested as possible sources (Maxwell 1990, pp. 292–94).

4.3 Chin textiles
John Barker

1   Bareigts 1981, p. 26, lists 66, but mentions neither Munn nor Lauktu. Several more may be assumed to exist given the confusion surrounding group labels and lack of fieldwork in southern areas particularly.
2   Diane Mott provided meticulous technical analysis and terminological advice.
3   Field interview, MVCP (Chin source), January 2002.
4   Field survey of Haka and Falam areas, STKP (Chin source), May 2002.
5   Field survey, NTT (Chin source), March–April 2002.

4.5 Karenic textiles
Sandra Dudley

1   Ornaments are also distinctive, with Kayan Kangkaw (Padaung) women being well-known for their brass neckrings, Kayah women for their black lacquered cotton legrings and large earplugs, etc. Bags and blankets too are characteristic Karenic items, although there is insufficient space to go into them here.
2   'Universal-style' avoids implying that so-called 'Western' items of clothing are new to or in some way exotic in Asian (and other) contexts. The adoption of such clothing is an insidious process rather than a sudden mass usage of another culture's style of garb.
3   Kayah men, for example, traditionally wore red shorts similar to the pair in the University of Oxford's Pitt Rivers Museum, collected before 1893 by H.G.A. Leveson (PRM number 1893.44.2).
4   In southern areas, frame looms have been used for many years.
5   This is a generalisation rather than a rule. The traditional clothing of Kayan Kang-nga (Yinbaw) women, for example, is similar in style to that of Kayah women, except that the predominant colour is not red but dark green or black. Fine white or yellow warp stripes are used for decoration, and the headcloth is decorated with blue and orange pompoms. Kayan Kang-nga men traditionally wore black or dark green knee-length shorts decorated all over with multicoloured tassels, 2 or 3 knee rings, a white shirt, and a white headcloth tied in a turban and decorated around the brow with multicoloured pompoms.
6   For versions of the 'python skin' legend explaining this pattern, see Fraser-Lu 1988, p. 95, Howard 1999, p. 71, Marshall 1997 (1922), p. 38.

4.6 Naga textiles
Vibha Joshi

1   Hutton 1921, p. 49.
2   Hutton 1969, p. 62.
3   Schneider 1987, Rowe 1981, Schevill 1985.

4.7 Shan State area textiles
Sandra Dudley

1   Early ethnographies/travel writings include Milne 1910, Woodthorpe 1897. See also Cameron 1912. Material on the Hmong, who are not discussed here, includes Clothing Culture Center 1993, Cohen 1987, Mallinson, Donnelly & Ly Hang 1988, John Michael Kohler Arts Center 1986, White 1982. On the Palaung, see Milne 1924 and Lowis 1906. On the Lisu, see Rose & Coggin Brown 1911. More generally, see Adams 1974, Howard, Wattanapun & Gordon 1997.

2   C.f. the 'Yang Lam' woman's top in the Bankfield Museum, Halifax (Howard 1999, p. 185).
3   See Milne 1924. See also the documentation, specifying clan, of the significant collection of Palaung textiles now in the Bankfield Museum in Halifax. Certainly, colour and pattern do still seem to vary by area. Palaung women in the Kalaw area, for example, in 1996 were observed by the author wearing slightly different skirtcloths to Palaung women in the Kengtung area; furthermore, the latter women wore silver waistrings over their skirtcloths, while those in the former area did not. Note however that names, locations and definitions of groups – be they ethnic, clan-based, etc. – can sometimes change not only over time, but also with whom one asks.
4   Hoods and leggings appear to be more typical of northern Palaungs than of those in southern and eastern Shan State. Personal communications in Shan State, 1996.
5   See Aye Aye Myint et al., 1971, and Maung Theikpa, 1968, both cited in Fraser-Lu 1988.
6   Fraser-Lu 1988, p. 97.

Chapter 5
Burma textiles in context

5.1 Burman court textiles in historical context
Frances Franklin

1   Thanks to Noel Singer for this attribution (Green Centre archive, letter dated 5 May 2001).
2   Franklin and Swallow 1994, p. 61.
3   Symes 1800, p. 31.
4   Yule 1858, preface (np).
5   Paothong Thonchua, personal communication, 1990.
6   Maxwell 1990, p. 176; Sen 1962.
7   Gupta 1991, pp. 138–39.
8   Singer 1994, p. 103.
9   N. Singer, letter 5 May 2001 (Green Centre Archives). Felice Beato, the Mandalay photographer owned an antiques shop where such items could be bought (N Singer, 1998, pp. 96–107).

5.2 Burmese textile texts: *sazigyo*
Ralph Isaacs

1   This essay would not have been begun without the help of weaver Peter Collingwood, nor completed without the computer expertise of Dr Tin Maung. I am deeply grateful to both.
2   Text weaving may have reached Burma from India via Arakan by the 18th century. The craft is said to have died out in Burma in the early 1970s (Singer 1993).
3   Scherman 1913.
4   Scherman 1913, p. 227, plate 3, and p. 232, plate 9.
5   Brighton commissioned from the master-weaver Peter Collingwood a detailed technical analysis of every tape (Collingwood 2000), which is the source of all the technical data given in this essay and indispensable for serious students of *sazigyo*. The definitive work on tablet weaving ancient and modern is Collingwood 1982.
6   Rarely, silk and metal thread are used in other *sazigyo*.
7   Singer 1993, p. 106, illustrates a brown-ground tape in the Royal Asiatic Society, London.
8   Scherman 1913, p. 232 and plate 10.
9   *Sazigyo* in Mon and in the Arakanese dialect of old Burmese are known, but the author knows of none in Shan. Most Shan manuscripts were written on paper, not palm leaves. No binding tape was needed for these folding books.
10 Another text (6 colours circa 1910 width 15 mm; private collection), reads: 'Businessman U Shway Do and wife Ma Aye and daughter Ma The Nu of Singapu Ward, Pazundaung, Rangoon paid the cost of writing this gilded manuscript of the *Tipitaka* and hope to attain Nirvana; they call on human and celestial beings to approve and applaud their deed of merit by calling out 'Thadu!' 'Well done!' The author is grateful to Dr Tan Bee Tin for checking the author's translation of this text.
11 The author is indebted to U Kyaw Zan Tha for translating the text of this *sazigyo*.
12 Personal communication, 1998.
13 Singer 1993, p. 103, suggests donors may have ordered that their birthday animal be included. But several birthday beasts, such as the *Naga* of Saturday-born people, do not occur on *sazigyo*.
14 Three small birds perched on the bell supports represent the three notes struck.
15 Staudigel 2000 gives many pictorial motifs from *sazigyo*, with patterns for modern tablet weavers to replicate them.

5.3 Design, meaning and identity in Naga textiles: continuity and change
Vibha Joshi

1   Green 1934, p. 9.
2   See Ao 1968, Barnes 1992, Joshi 1994, 2000, and Shirali 1983 for analyses of social cultural aspects of Naga textile production.
3   Jacobs 1990, p. 177.
4   Fürer-Haimendorf 1976, p. 46.
5   Hutton, tour diary, 15 June 1934.
6   J.P. Mills Collection item 1928.69.1543, Pitt Rivers Museum, University of Oxford.
7   Joshi 2000, p. 10.

5.4 Clothing and courtship: Akha textiles in social context
Mika Toyota

1   Alting von Geusau 2000.
2   See Toyota 1996.
3   See Kammerer 1988.
4   Personal communication, 1996.

5.5 Textiles in exile: Karenni refugees in Thailand
Sandra Dudley

1   I am eternally grateful to my Karenni refugee friends for their patience, and generosity with both their time and knowledge. Thanks are due too to the bodies who supported my research: Jesus College, Oxford; the Emslie Horniman and RAI/Sutasoma funds of the Royal Anthropological Institute; the Peter Lienhardt Memorial Fund, University of Oxford; the Cha Fund, University of Oxford; the Board of Graduate Studies, University of Oxford; and the Evans Fund, University of Cambridge.
2   Parts of this chapter have previously appeared in Dudley 2000 and Dudley 2002; for an examination of the impact of dress and textile issues on refugee welfare, see Dudley 1999.
3   In 2002, it stands at around 25,000.
4   They are also transitional in other ways. See Dudley 2000 & Dudley forthcoming.
5   By 'not as good', they mean that the loom is not as comfortable to use and that the strap does not last as long. They are not referring to the quality of textile produced.
6   Nonetheless, for a good number of villages such full-scale cotton and textile production was practised within the last few decades, even if it is no longer the norm. Naw Sarah (name changed), for example, a Paku woman in her late forties, said women in her village of origin had grown, prepared and dyed their own cotton within her adult lifetime. She added, however, that this was no longer the case.
7   Dudley 2002.

Chapter 6
Burma textiles in wider contexts: collecting, commissioning, research

6.1 Documenting Chin textiles
John Barker

1   Special thanks to my talented Chin researchers: MKVP, NTT and STKP. Thanks also to Kate Fitz Gibbon, Roger Hollander, Susan Lander, Mary Jane Leland, R. Weldon and the Southeast Asian Collection library staff at Northern Illinois University.
2   Much of the new material from this area in the Green collection fits exactly this description. It was collected in Rangoon in 1997 and 1999, and includes some good pieces but is poorly provenanced (see Fig.6.1.ii and iii).
3   The first published Chin textile field study was distributed in 2001 (Garner and Bommer 1999–2000).
4   In particular, see Parry 1932, Carey and Tuck 1896, Lehman 1963, Stevenson 1943.
5   Many peoples called 'Chin' today prefer the term 'Zo' but the issue is unresolved. I have retained 'Chin' for clarity.
6   U Ba Myaing 1934, p. 127.

6.2 Collecting Shan textiles and their stories
Lisa Maddigan

1   In 1935, E. T. D. Gaudoin sent James Green 'The Small Haka Chin Vocabulary Handbook', that he had written for the use of members of the Burma Frontiers Association interested in the Haka dialect of the Chin language.
2   Eleanor Gaudoin has also carried out oral history work with the Imperial War Museum in 1996.
3   Furthermore, Sao Hseng U was well acquainted with British colonial society, and had lived in England from 1929 to 1932 with E. T. D. Gaudoin.
4   Quote taken from a letter of recommendation written by James Green for Sao Hkam Hip Hpa in August 1948 (Green Centre archives).
5   *Ibid.*

6.3.1 Making textiles in Myitkyina, 2001–2
Lisa Maddigan

1   For full documentation of the commissioning process, and related Kachin oral history and archive work, see the Green Centre archive. The Museum is grateful to Sadan Ja Ngai who co-ordinated the textile project in Myitkyina, and to Salaw Zau Ring, Htoi Awng, Hkanhpa Tu Sadan, Mandy Sadan, and Kha Lum.

2   While this was considered a 'representative' set by the project participants, there are many variations in dress styles within the groups represented, and other Kachin groups not included in the project. For example, the Nung Lungmi, who are often grouped together with the Rawang people, have a strong sense of individual group identity. In recognition of this, the Nung Lungmi Cultural Committee donated a male and female outfit to the Museum in March 2002, the styles of which differ from the Rawang outfits made for the project (see Fig.6.3.2.vi).

3   The definition of 'traditional' dress plays a significant role in distinguishing and displaying Kachin group identity in Kachin State (see Sadan, below). For example, displays of traditional Kachin dress and weaving techniques form part of the *manau* festival, an important cultural event organised by the Kachin community (Sadan 2002). The textile project includes records of dress at the *manau* in Myitkyina, December 2001 (Green archive). Exhibits of traditional dress also feature in the museum in Myitkyina, and although the displays in this government-run museum seemed not to be highly regarded by people working on the project in Myitkyina, the connection between museums and traditional dress was not unprecedented. However, many of the weavers were intrigued by why a museum in England was so interested in Kachin textiles. Part of the intention of the project was to develop a better understanding of the Museum's motives. To this end, extensive information about Green, his collection and the Green Centre's work was prepared for the people working on the commission in Myitkyina. Consent forms were prepared for each of the weavers to sign, clearly outlining the intentions of the project and how the objects and documentation would be used. All written information was translated into Jinghpaw, the Kachin people's main language.

4   The script developed for Jinghpaw by Baptist missionaries in the 19th century is widely considered by Jinghpaw speakers to be inadequate, particularly in the lack of tone markers. This means that written Jinghpaw transcripts can be awkward or misleading. Great effort is being made in Kachin State to develop a new improved script for the Jinghpaw language (Mandy Sadan, personal communication, 2002).

6.3.2 Textile contexts in Kachin State
Mandy Sadan

1   The pre-colonial Burmese State also attempted to codify the names of groups in and around its borders. However, the argument here assumes that the political and social nature of this was different to that introduced by the British colonial authorities (1826–1948), which constructed ethnicity around western concepts of 'race' and had different implications and effects. See Sadan, forthcoming.

2   OIOC [Oriental & India Office Collections, British Library] – Fort William Political Consultations, 15 February 1836, No. 41.

3   Hannay 1847.

4   *The Kachin Hills Manual*, 1924.

5   See *Linguistic Survey of Burma*, 1917, and *Census of India*, 1911 for the sometimes contradictory ways in which different subgroups were related to the identity Kachin. See Enriquez 1920, for an account of early recruitment in the Indian Army of young men from different Kachin subgroups.

6   Brown 1837; OIOC – Fort William Political Consultations, 15 February, 1836, No. 41.

7   Hannay 1847.

8   Deb 1979.

9   Woodman 1962.

10 *The Nation*, 15 February 1955, Rangoon. For further information on the way that ethno-political relations between Jinghpaw and Naga communities in the Shingbwiyang area were manipulated by the British administration, see Sadan 2002.

11 Enriquez 1923.

12 *Ibid.*

13 Jemadar Kolu Tu 1924. Enriquez 1920, relates that after the Mesopotamia Campaign of the First World War in 1918 the bags of Kachin soldiers killed in action were returned to their families so that the final funeral rituals could be held according to local custom.

14 OIOC: M/5/14, B(P)187, 30 Jun–6 Jul 1939 – Kachin Regeneration Campaign: 'Record of Proceedings of a Conference held in

Maymyo on October 23rd, 25th & 26th to consider the Question of the Alleged Deterioration of the Kachin Race and Measures to be taken to arrest it'; M/3/563, B7519/38, Nov 1938 – Sept 1939: 'Kachin Tribes – Proposed visit of G. A. J. Teasdale to Burma to study the medical cause of the decline of the Kachins'.

15 Jemadar Kolu Tu 1924.

16 Armed Kachin opposition began in 1961, but other communities, such as some Karen peoples, have been in arms against the government from 1948 until the present day. See Smith 1999 for an overview of the modern history of ethnic conflict in Burma.

17 Sadan 2002.

18 C.f. Dudley 2000, and Chapter 3, this volume.

19 *The Nation*, Rangoon, 12 February 1952.

20 OIOC: M/4/2811, B/F&FA 3/46(vii), Jun 1945 – May 1947: Frontier Areas – relations between Frontier Areas and Ministerial Burma – Panglong Conference.

21 *The Nation*, Rangoon, 12 February 1952.

22 Smith 1999.

23 See Khin Aung Tin 1991; 'Union Day, February 12th, 2000 – Message from U Aung Shwe, Chairman of National League for Democracy and Message from U Lwin, A Central Executive Member of the National League for Democracy'; 'Statement of Chin National Front on the 55th Anniversary of Union Day, Central Committee, Chin National Front, 12 February 2002'; and *The Irrawaddy*, February 2002.

24 Daw Aung San Suu Kyi 1996, gives an account of an alternative Union Day festival held by the National League for Democracy, the main opposition to the government, which also focuses on dances and representations of traditional dress but which seeks to give these different political meanings

25 See Sadan 2000 for further discussion of these contemporary responses to ethnic stereotyping and notions of development.

26 My thanks to Sitthipong Samathimankong for bringing this figure to my attention and to Dashi Naw and Gwi Kai Nan for their comments.

27 This trend continues today. One of the busiest dance troupes performing outside the formal state stage is that of Wunpawng Ningja. Sarama Tawng Ra takes great care in designing the modern/traditional costumes of the troupe. The designs are then publicised further through the production of a calendar, which is very popular as

decorative wall sheets in most
Kachin homes.

28 In recent years, this kind of men's skirtcloth
has become associated with support for
Daw Aung San Suu Kyi's National League
for Democracy (NLD). However, some
Kachin men in the urban areas of lower
Burma find this can create difficulties for
them at times of political unrest. An
assumption is automatically made by the
authorities at such times that they must be
NLD supporters, when for many the
primary reference they are making by
wearing this skirtcloth is to their Kachin
identity, which is in itself sometimes a
statement of opposition but cannot be
simplistically equated with supporting
the NLD.

29 Arnold 1897. *The Nation*, 1952.

30 *Ibid*. In his dissertation for Cambridge
University 'The Tribes of Upper Burma
North of 24° Latitude and their
Classification' (1934), J. H. Green wrote also
of what he considered an innate difference
in aesthetic responses to colour in dress
between those communities lying on the
east and on the west of the Nmai River in
what is today Kachin State: 'It is particularly
noticeable how the Hkahkus favour sober
colours and little jewellery whereas the
Nmai people love bright colours and
innumerable bright coloured necklaces'
(p.65). In Green's analysis, the issue of
access to bazaars was not raised. Hkahku
women did not travel to markets. Trade
was carried out only by Hkahku men and
this represents an important difference in
gender roles in various areas of the Kachin
hills. The aesthetic preferences for greater
and lesser colour can still be seen to some
extent in the costumes produced in the
recent project.

31 *Prospectus of the Saunders Weaving Institute,
Amarapura*, 1937.

32 My thanks to Dashi Naw and Sa Tu Ja Lai
for their comments.

33 The decision to weave the two-piece
contemporary style suit on a mechanical
loom as opposed to a backstrap loom was
problematic for several reasons. A big loom
has to be specially set up for a particular
design, an expensive and time consuming
process. For this reason, the cloth is woven
in large quantities, rather than for a single
outfit as with hand woven material. The
tailored design of the two piece suit does
not allow for the narrow width of fabric
woven on a backstrap loom and would
have to have been made from two lengths
of material sewn together, leaving the suit

with an unsightly seam. Also, most weavers
working on big looms in Myitkyina are
Burman, and Sadan Ja Ngai was keen for all
weavers working on the project to be
Kachin, because of their understanding of
Kachin designs. Fortunately Sadan Ja Ngai
found a loom owner who was willing to
have one of her big looms set up for this
project and Sa Tu Ja Lai, a Kachin weaver
skilled in both hand and machine weaving,
agreed to weave the designs. The fabric
was then cut and made into an elegant suit
and handbag by U Thwin tailors
in Myitkyina.

Appendix: Museum collections of textiles from Burma

Sandra Dudley

1 I am grateful for all the help extended to
me by staff at the museums mentioned,
particularly at those I was able to visit.

2 Thanks to the Burma Project of the Open
Society Institute, who funded most of the
research.

3 I used Blackburn 1994 as a starting point.

4 The most important colonial collections
are obviously in Great Britain, while the
most extensive missionary collections are
in North America.

5 Howard 1999, p. 9, suggests that the most
relevant collection in Burma is the Shan
State Museum in Taunggyi.

6 An important proviso is that in practice,
many museum objects are wrongly, too
narrowly, too vaguely identified, or not
identified at all. A particularly common
misidentification is the labelling of Karen
Job's tear-decorated and embroidered
tunics as 'Kachin'. See also the discussion of
categorising textiles in chapter 3 of this
volume.

7 For a discussion of Green's photographs
and some other archive photographs of
Burma, see Dell (ed.) 2000.

8 See chapter 3, this volume. More generally,
on 'type' photographs see Edwards 1990.

9 See Innes 1957, Roth 1901, Start 1917.

10 See Hansen 1960.

Glossary

1 Noel Singer, letter 5 May 2001 (Green
Centre Archives).

2 Fraser-Lu 1994, p. 263.

3 *Ibid*.

4 *Ibid*.

Bibliography

M. Adams, 'Dress and design among the peoples of highland southeast Asia', *The Textile Museum Journal*, 4, no. 1, 1974, pp. 51–66

L. Alting von Geusau, 'Akha internal history: marginalization and the ethnic alliance system', in A. Turton (ed.), *Civility and Savagery: Social Identity in Tai States*, Richmond, Surrey (Curzon) 2000

A. Ao, *The Arts and Crafts of Nagaland*, Kohima (Naga Institute of Culture, Government of Nagaland) 1968

G. F. Arnold, *Monograph on Cotton Fabrics and the Cotton Industry in Burma*, Rangoon (Government Printing) 1897

Aung San Suu Kyi, 'Letter from Burma (no.16) – dancing under the banner of ethnic harmony – Union Day dances', *Mainichi Daily News*, 11 March 1996

Aye Aye Myint et al., 'The structure and designs of Zin-me silk of the Shan States of Burma', unpublished BE thesis, Rangoon Institute of Technology, 1971

M. Banks, *Ethnicity: Anthropological Constructions*, London (Routledge) 1996

A. Bareigts, *Les Lautu, Contribution à l'étude de l'organisation sociale d'une Ethnie Chin de Haute-Birmanie*, Selaf (CNRS) 1981

R. Barnes, 'Women as headhunters: the making and meaning of textiles in a southeast Asian context', in R. Barnes and J.B. Eicher (eds.), *Dress and Gender: Making and Meaning in Cultural Contexts*, Oxford (Berg) 1992, pp. 29–43

R. Barnes and J. B. Eicher, *Dress and Gender: Making and Meaning in Cultural Contexts*, Oxford (Berg) 1992

R. H. Barnes, 'Introduction', in R. H. Barnes, A. Gray & B. Kingsbury (eds.), *Indigenous Peoples of Asia*, Ann Arbor (Association for Asian Studies) 1995

T. Blackburn, *A Report on the Location of Burmese Artefacts in Museums*, Gartmore (Kiscadale) 1994

N. Brown, 'The Singpo language', *Journal of the Asiatic Society of Bengal*, Calcutta, 1837

A. A. Cameron, *A Note on the Palaungs of the Kodaung Hill Tracts of the Mong Mit State*, Rangoon (Government Printing) 1912

B. S. Carey and H. N. Tuck, *The Chin Hills: a History of the People, our Dealings with Them, their Customs and Manners, and a Gazetteer of their Country*, Vol. I, Rangoon (Superintendent, Government Printing) 1896

Census of India 1911: Volume IX – Burma, Part 1 – Report, Rangoon (Government Printing) 1912

M. Chapman, '"Freezing the frame": dress and ethnicity in Brittany and Gaelic Scotland', in J. B. Eicher (ed.), *Dress and Ethnicity*, Oxford (Berg) 1995

Clothing Culture Center, *Miao Textile Design*, Taipei (Fu Jen University Press) 1993

E. Cohen, 'The Hmong cross: a cosmic symbol in Hmong (Meo) textile designs', *Res*, Autumn 1987, pp. 27–45

P. Collingwood, *The Techniques of Tablet Weaving*, London (Faber) 1982 and McMinnville, Oregon (Robin and Russ Handweavers Inc.) 1996

P. Collingwood, 'Detailed technical report on the Burmese manuscript binding tapes in the Brighton Museum', unpublished manuscript, James Green Centre for World Art (Brighton Museum and Art Gallery) 2000

K. Deb, *Impact of Plantations on the Agrarian Structure of the Brahmaputra Valley*, Calcutta (Occasional Paper No.24, Centre for Studies in Social Sciences) 1979

E. Dell (ed.), *Burma Frontier Photographs 1918–1935*, Brighton and London (James Green Centre for World Art and Merrell Publishers) 2000

S. Dudley, 'Burmese collections in the Pitt Rivers Museum: an introduction', *Journal of Museum Ethnography*, 5, 1996, pp. 57–64

S. Dudley, '"Traditional" culture and refugee welfare in north-west Thailand', *Forced Migration Review*, 6, 1999, pp. 5–8

S. Dudley, 'Displacement and identity: Karenni refugees in Thailand', unpublished DPhil thesis, University of Oxford, 2000

S. Dudley, 'Appropriating and transforming "tradition": Karenni dress in exile', in R. Blurton & A. Green (eds.), *Burma – Art and Archaeology*, London (British Museum Press) 2002

D. Durham, 'The lady in the logo: tribal dress and Western culture in a southern African community', in J. B. Eicher (ed.), *Dress and Ethnicity*, Oxford (Berg) 1995

E. Edwards, 'Photographic "types": the pursuit of method', *Visual Anthropology*, 3, nos. 2–3, 1990, pp. 235–58

J. Eicher (ed.), *Dress and Ethnicity*, Oxford (Berg) 1995

C. M. Enriquez, *Races of Burma*, Delhi (Manager of Publications) 1933 (first published Meiktila 1920)

C. M. Enriquez, *A Burmese Arcady: an Account of a Long & Intimate Sojourn amongst the Mountain Dwellers of the Burmese Hinterland & of their Engaging Characteristics and Customs*, London (Seeley Service & Co.) 1923

F. Franklin and D. Swallow, 'Identifying with the gods', *The 1994 Hali Annual*, 1, 1994, pp. 48–61

S. Fraser-Lu, *Handwoven Textiles of Southeast Asia*, Singapore (Oxford University Press) 1988

S. Fraser-Lu, *Burmese Crafts: Past and Present*, Singapore (Oxford University Press) 1994

J. Friedman, 'Narcissism, roots, and postmodernity: the constitution of selfhood in global crisis', in S. Lash & J. Friedman (eds.), *Modernity and Identity*, Oxford (Basil Blackwell) 1992

C. V. Fürer-Haimendorf, *Return to the Naked Nagas: An Anthropologist's View of Nagaland 1936–1970*, London (John Murray) 1976

D. L. Garner and J. Bommer, 'Notes from the field: on the trail of Khumi, Khami, and Mro Textiles', *The Textile Museum Journal*, 38–39, 1999–2000, pp. 27–42

J. Goodman, *Meet the Akhas*, Bangkok (White Lotus) 1996

J. H. Green, 'The tribes of upper Burma north of 24° latitude and their classification', unpublished dissertation, University of Cambridge 1934

C. S. Gupta, 'The gilded thread', *The India Magazine*, 12, 1991, pp. 138–39

R. Handler and J. Linnekin, 'Tradition, genuine or spurious', *Journal of American Folklore*, 97, 1984, pp. 273–90

S. F. Hannay, *Sketch of the Singphos or the Kakhyens of Burma: the Position of this Tribe as Regards Baumo, and the Inland Trade of the Valley of the Irrawaddy with Yunnan and their Connection with the North-eastern Frontier of Assam*, Calcutta (Military Orphan Press) 1847

H. H. Hansen, *Some Costumes of Highland Burma at the Ethnographical Museum of Gothenburg*, Göteborg (Etnografiska Museet) 1960

E. Hobsbawm, 'Introduction: inventing traditions', in E. Hobsbawm & T. Ranger (eds.), *The Invention of Tradition*, Cambridge (Cambridge University Press) 1983

M. C. Howard, *Textiles of the Hill Tribes of Burma*, Bangkok (White Lotus) 1999

M. C. Howard, W. Wattanapun and A. Gordon (eds.), *Traditional T'ai Arts in Contemporary Perspective*, Bangkok (White Lotus) 1997

J. H. Hutton, *The Sema Nagas*, London (Macmillan and Co.) 1921

J. H. Hutton, 'Tour diaries of District Commissioner Naga Hills, Assam, June–July 1934', unpublished manuscript, J.H. Hutton Box 3, Pitt Rivers Museum Archives, University of Oxford, 1934

J. H. Hutton, *The Angami Nagas*, Bombay (Oxford University Press) 1969 (first published 1921)

R. A. Innes, *Costumes of Upper Burma and the Shan States in the Collections of Bankfield Museum*, Halifax (Halifax Museums) 1957

J. Jacobs, *The Nagas: Hill Peoples of Northeast India, Society, Culture and the Colonial Encounter*, London (Thames and Hudson) 1990

Jemadar Kolu Tu, 'Jinghpaw ni a bu hpun palawng hking lailen a lam', *Jinghpaw Shi Laika*, Rangoon (American Baptist Mission Press), November 1924

John Michael Kohler Arts Center, *Hmong Art: Tradition and Change*, Sheboygan, Wisconsin (John Michael Kohler Arts Center) 1986

V. Joshi, 'Handicrafts of Nagaland', New Delhi (manuscript project report for the Development Commissioner for Handicrafts, Ministry of Textiles) 1994

V. Joshi, 'Naga textiles – today', *Oxford Asian Textile Group Newsletter*, 15, February 2000, pp. 7–10

C. A. Kammerer, 'Shifting gender asymmetries among Akha of northern Thailand', in N. Eberharat (ed.), *Gender, Power and the Construction of the Moral Order: Studies from the Thai Periphery*, Madison (University of Wisconsin) 1988, pp. 33–51

Khin Aung Tin, *The Working People's Daily*, Rangoon, 12 February 1991

B. M. Knauft, 'Gender identity, political economy and modernity in Melanesia and Amazonia', *Journal of the Royal Anthropological Institute*, 3, no. 2, 1997, pp. 233–59

F.K. Lehman, *The Structure of Chin Society*, Urbana, IL (University of Illinois Press) 1963

P. Lewis and E. Lewis, *Peoples of the Golden Triangle: Six Tribes in Thailand*, London (Thames and Hudson) 1984

H. Ling Roth, 'Bankfield Museum notes no. II – the Burmese collection no. I', *The Halifax Naturalist*, 6, 1901

Linguistic Survey of Burma: Preparatory Stage of Linguistic Census, Rangoon (Government Printing) 1917

C. C. Lowis, *A Note on the Palaungs of Hsipaw and Tawpeng, Ethnographical Survey of India, Burma, No. 1*, Rangoon (Government Printing) 1906

S. Macdonald, *Reimagining Culture. Histories, Identities and the Gaelic Renaissance*, Oxford (Berg) 1997

H. I. Marshall, *The Karen People of Burma: a Study in Anthropology and Ethnology*, Bangkok (White Lotus) 1997 (first published 1922)

Maung Theikpa, 'Textiles from Inle Lake', *Forward*, 6, no. 24, 1968, pp. 16–20

J. Mallinson, N. Donnelly and Ly Hang, *Hmong Batik: a Textile Technique from Laos*, Seattle (Mallinson/Informations Services) 1988

R. Maxwell, *Textiles of Southeast Asia: Tradition, Trade and Transformation*, Melbourne (Oxford University Press) 1990

L. (or M. L.) Milne, *Shans at Home*, London (John Murray) 1910

L. (or M.L.) Milne, *The Home of an Eastern Clan: a Study of the Palaungs of the Shan States*, Oxford (Clarendon Press) 1924

Mi Mi Gyi (Shwebo Mi Mi Gyi), *Pay Sa Htouk Cho Hma Hsu Taung Sa Mya* (Collected Texts of Manuscript Binding Tapes), Rangoon (Sarpay Beikman) 1993

D. Odo, 'Anthropological boundaries and photographic frontiers: J. H. Green's visual language of salvage', in E. Dell (ed.), *Burma Frontier Photographs 1918–1935*, Brighton and London (James Green Centre for World Art and Merrell Publishers) 2000, pp. 41–49

N. E. Parry, *The Lakhers*, Mizoram (Tribal Research Institute) 1976 (first published 1932)

Prospectus of the Saunders Weaving Institute, Amarapura, Rangoon (Government Printing) 1937

A. Rose and J. Coggin Brown, 'Lisu (Yawyin) tribes of the Burma-China frontier', *Memoirs of the Royal Asiatic Society of Bengal*, 3, 1911, pp. 249–77

A. P. Rowe, *A Century of Change in Guatemalan Textiles*, New York (Center for Inter-American Relations) 1981

M. Sadan, 'The Kachin photographs in the J.H. Green collection: a contemporary context', in *Burma Frontier Photoraphs: 1918–1935*, Brighton and London (Green Centre for Non-Western Art and Merrell Publishers) 2000, pp. 51–65

M. Sadan, 'The Kachin manau and manau shading – development of an ethno-cultural symbol', in R. Blurton & A. Green (eds.), *Burma – Art and Archaeology*, London (British Museum Press) 2002

M. Sadan, 'Decolonising identity – the problem of "Kachin"', unpublished PhD thesis, SOAS, University of London, forthcoming

L. Scherman, 'Brettchenwebereien aus Birma und den Himalayalandern', *Jahrbuch für Bildenden Kunst*, 8, 1913, pp. 223–42

M. B. Schevill, *Evolution of Textile Design from the Highlands of Guatemala*, Berkeley (Lowie Museum of Anthropology) 1985

J. Schneider, 'The anthropology of cloth', *Annual Review of Anthropology*, 16, 1987, pp. 409–48

J. G. Scott and J. P. Hardiman, *Gazetteer of Upper Burma and the Shan States*, Vol. 1, Pts. 1 & II, Rangoon (Government Printing) 1900

S. P. Sen, 'The role of Indian textiles in southeastern trade in the 17th century', *Journal of Southeast Asian History*, 3, no. 2, 1962, pp. 92–110

Y. J. Seng and B. Wass, 'Traditional Palestinian wedding dress as a symbol of nationalism', in J. B. Eicher (ed.), *Dress and Ethnicity*, Oxford (Berg) 1995

A. Shirali, *Textile and Bamboo Crafts of the Northeastern Region*, Shillong (National Institute of Design, Northeastern Council) 1983

N. F. Singer, 'Kammavaca texts, their covers and binding ribbons', *Arfs of Asia*, 23, no. 3, 1993, pp. 97–106

N. F. Singer, 'Maha Bandula the Younger; Burmese court costumes in the West', *Arts of Asia*, 24, no. 6, 1994

N. F. Singer, 'Felice Beato's Burmese days', *Arts of Asia*, 28, no. 5, 1998, pp. 96–107

M. Smith, *Burma: Insurgency and the Politics of Ethnicity*, London (Zed Books) 1999 (first published 1991)

L. Start, *Burmese Textiles from the Shan and Kachin Districts*, Halifax (Bankfield Museum) 1917

O. Staudigel, *Der Zauber des Brettchenwebens* (Tablet Weaving Magic: Patterns from Oriental Countries), Krefeld (Libri Books) 2001

H. N. C. Stevenson, *The Economics of the Central Chin Tribes*, Bombay (Times of India Press) 1943

M. Symes, *An Account of an Embassy to the Kingdom of Ava, Sent by the Governor General of India in the Year 1795*, London (Nicol and Wright) 1800, reprinted Farnborough (Gregg International Ltd.) 1969

The Irrawaddy, 'Burma's ethnic groups banned from celebrations', *The Irrawaddy*, Chiang Mai, February 2002

The Kachin Hills Manual, Rangoon (Government Printing) 1924

The Nation, Rangoon, 24 January 1952

The Nation, Rangoon, 15 February 1955

C. Toren, 'Making the present, revealing the past: the mutability and continuity of tradition as process', *Man* (N.S.), 23, no. 4, 1988, pp. 696–717

M. Toyota, 'The Akha courtship journey and social change', *Research Report No. 4*, Tokyo (Japanese Institute for the Study of Mobility and Culture) 1996, pp. 111–18 (in Japanese)

U Ba Myaing, 'The northern hills of the Ponnagyun township', *Journal of the Burma Research Society*, 23, part III, 1934, pp. 128–30

V. White, *Pa Ndau: the Needlework of the Hmong*, Cheney (Cheney Free Press) 1982

F. Wilson and B. F. Frederiksen, 'Introduction: studies in ethnicity, gender and the subversion of nationalism', in F. Wilson & B.F. Frederiksen (eds.), *Ethnicity, Gender and the Subversion of Nationalism*, London (Frank Cass & Co., Ltd.) 1995

D. Woodman, *The Making of Burma*, London (Cresset Press) 1962

R. G. Woodthorpe, 'Some accounts of the Shans and hill tribes of the states on the Mekong', *Journal of the Royal Anthropological Institute of Great Britain and Ireland*, 26, 1897, pp. 13–28

H. Yule, *A Narrative of the Mission of the Governor General of India to the Court of Ava in 1855*, London (Smith Elder & Co.) 1858

Selected further reading

J. T. Bailey, 'Burmese textiles', *Burma Art Newsletter*, Denison University, 1, no. 4, 1969, p. 5

J. P. Barbier, *Art of Nagaland*, Geneva (Musée Barbier-Müeller) 1985

D. K. Burnham, *Warp and Weft: a Textile Terminology*, Toronto (Royal Ontario Museum) 1980

China Art Publishing Company (ed.), *Costumes of the Minority Peoples of China*, Kyoto (Binobi) 1982

Chira Cogkol, 'Textiles and costumes in Thailand', *Arts of Asia*, 12, no. 6, 1982

Y. Y. Chung, *The Art of Oriental Embroidery: History, Aesthetics and Techniques*, New York (Charles Scribner's Sons) 1983

S. Conway, *Thai Textiles*, London (British Museum Press) 1992

S. Fraser-Lu, 'Kalagas, Burmese wall hangings and related embroideries', *Arts of Asia*, July–August 1982, pp. 73–82

E. M. Hinton, 'The dress of the Pwo Karen of north Thailand', *Journal of the Siam Society*, 62, 1974, pp. 27–34

Y. Hokari, 'The Buddhist robes in Japan, Korea, China and Burma', *Proceedings of the Fifth Asian Costume Congress*, Tokyo (International Association of Costume) 1986, pp. 172–73

Maung Pe Kywe, 'Woven with 100 shuttles', *Forward*, 3, no. 6, 1994, pp. 11–16

H. Puls, *The Art of Cutwork and Applique*, Newton Center (Charles T. Bradford Co.) 1978

San Win, 'Robes for the Buddha, Burma: golden country', *Horizons Magazine*, no date, p. 15

J.G. Scott, *Burma: A Handbook of Practical Information*, London (Alexander Moring Ltd.) 1911

E. Shears and D. Fielding, *Appliqué*, New York (Watson-Gupthill) 1972

M. A. Stanislaw, *Kalagas: the Wall Hangings of Southeast Asia*, Menlo Park, California (Ainslie's), 1987

A.B. Weiner and J. Schneider (eds.), *Cloth and Human Experience*, Washington & London (Smithsonian Institute Press) 1989

E. B. Willis, 'The textile arts of India's north-east borderlands', *Arts of Asia*, 17, no. 1, 1987

Index